An Imaginary Racism

For Patrice Champion, in memory of
Belgrade and Sarajevo

Pascal Bruckner

An Imaginary Racism
Islamophobia and Guilt

Translated by Steven Rendall and Lisa Neal

polity

First published in French as *Un racisme imaginaire. Islamophobie et culpabilité*
© Éditions Grasset & Fasquelle, 2017

This English edition © Polity Press, 2022

Polity Press
65 Bridge Street
Cambridge CB2 1UR, UK

Polity Press
101 Station Landing
Suite 300
Medford, MA 02155, USA

ISBN-13: 978-1-5095-3064-9
ISBN-13: 978-1-5095-5490-4 (pb)

A catalogue record for this book is available from the British Library.

Library of Congress Cataloging-in-Publication Data
Names: Bruckner, Pascal, author.
Title: An imaginary racism : Islamophobia and guilt / Pascal Bruckner.
Other titles: Racisme imaginaire. English
Description: Medford, MA, USA : Polity, [2018] | Includes bibliographical references and index.
Identifiers: LCCN 2018001630 (print) | LCCN 2018029268 (ebook) | ISBN 9781509530663 (Epub) | ISBN 9781509530649 (hardback)
Subjects: LCSH: Islam--Public opinion. | Islamophobia--Western countries. | Islam--Western countries. | Islamic fundamentalism--Western countries. | Islam and politics--Western countries. | Political correctness--Western countries. | Racism--Western countries. | Western countries--Ethnic relations.
Classification: LCC BP52 (ebook) | LCC BP52 .B7813 2018 (print) | DDC 305.6/97--dc23
LC record available at https://lccn.loc.gov/2018001630

Typeset in 11 on 13 pt Sabon
by Fakenham Prepress Solutions, Fakenham, Norfolk NR21 8NL
Printed and bound in Great Britain by TJ Books Ltd, Padstow, Cornwall

For further information on Polity, visit our website: politybooks.com

Contents

A Note on the Text

This book is the outcome of many articles published since 2003 in Le Figaro, Le Monde, and Libération. I devoted about a dozen pages of The Tyranny of Guilt (Princeton University Press, 2010) to Islamophobia. I have also included here a lecture given at Indiana University, Bloomington, in 2012, and at Yale, on the inversion of the debt between anti-Semitism and Islamophobia. This lecture was published in English by Indiana University Press in 2015 in an essay collection edited by Alvin Rosenfeld under the title Deciphering the New Anti-Semitism. It appeared in France in the Revue des Deux Mondes in June 2014.

A new word had been created to
help the blind remain blind:
Islamophobia. To criticize the
militant stridency of this religion in
its contemporary incarnation was to
be a bigot.

Salman Rushdie, Joseph Anton

Introduction

A Semantic Rejuvenation

In 1910, André Quellien, a writer working for the French minister of the colonies, published a work entitled *Muslim Politics in French West Africa*.[1] Addressed to specialists and imperial officials, it offers moderate praise for the religion of the Quran as 'practical and indulgent', and better adapted to the 'natives', whereas Christianity is 'too complicated, too abstract, too austere for the rudimentary, materialistic mentality of the negro'. The author of this report thought it important to emphasize that so long as it was treated tactfully, Islam would become French colonialism's best ally and favour European influence and control. Because the religion of the Prophet 'wrests these peoples away from fetishism and its degrading practices', Quellien argued that it was imperative to stop seeing Islam as fanaticism and to treat it instead with a benevolent neutrality, thus foreshadowing the great Arabist Louis Massignon

(1883–1962), a left-wing Catholic who specialized in Muslim mysticism and advocated dialogue between Islam and the Roman Catholic Church. Thus Quellien denounced the 'Islamophobia' that was rampant among colonial officials, but he was just as opposed to the 'Islamophilia' peculiar to Romantic orientalism: 'singing the praises of Islam is just as biased as describing it unjustly'. Islam must be objectively considered as a tool for governing. Here, Quellien writes as an administrator concerned about social peace: he deplores the temptation to demonize a religion that keeps the peace in the empire, no matter what abuses – minor ones, in his view – it may commit, such as the continuing practices of slavery and polygamy. Since Islam is colonialism's best ally, its followers must be protected from the harmful influence of modern ideas and their ways of life must be respected (an attitude found today on the far left and in English-speaking countries).

During the same period, Maurice Delafosse, another colonial official residing in Dakar, wrote: 'Whatever may be said by those for whom Islamophobia is a principle of governing natives, France has nothing more to fear from Muslims than from non-Muslims in West Africa [...]. Thus Islamophobia has no more *raison d'être* in West Africa, where, on the other hand, Islamophilia (in the sense of a preference granted Muslims) is said to create a feeling of distrust among non-Muslim peoples, who are the most numerous.'[2]

Islamophobia: the term probably already existed in the nineteenth century, which explains its spontaneous use by imperial officials. As for its antonym, Islamophilia, whether erudite or popular, since the seventeenth century it has been a constant in European history, which is still massively fascinated by Islamic civilization.[3] But after the Iranian Revolution of 1980 the expression 'Islamophobia' underwent a mutation that weaponized it. Between the expulsion of the American feminist Kate Millet from Teheran in 1979 for having protested against the regime's requirement that Iranian women wear a veil, and the Rushdie affair in 1988, which exploded under the influence of British Muslims, this dormant word suddenly awoke and became active in another form. A word does not belong to the person who created it but to the one who reinvented it to make its use widespread. This lexical rejuvenation makes it possible to kill two birds with one stone: stigmatizing traitors to the Muslim faith, on the one hand, and shutting up godless Westerners, on the other.

In 1789 and again in 1791, France abolished the crime of blasphemy, which had caused centuries of conflicts between Catholics and Protestants (the Restoration later reinstituted another law against sacrilege that was intended above all to muzzle the press, but it was repealed during the July Monarchy and definitively abrogated in July 1881). In his report on the planned penal code, a member of the Constituent Assembly, Lepeletier de Saint-Fargeau, wrote that it was necessary 'to get rid of this crowd of imaginary crimes swelling the old collections of our laws. You will no longer find in them the great crimes of heresy, lèse-majesté, sorcery, or practising magic, for which, in the name of the divine, so much blood has soiled the earth'.[4] A magnificent proposal that might seem outdated today if so many obscurantist forces, led by UN-accredited lawyers and theologians from the Middle East, were not doing all they can to revive this crime of blasphemy, this 'oral crime' that challenged the social and cosmic order and that under the Old Regime was often punished, in France and in Europe, by cutting off the offender's tongue, sewing his mouth shut, or even torturing and killing him. In the spirit of Lepeletier de Saint-Fargeau ridiculing blasphemy, we might describe the accusation of 'Islamophobia' as 'imaginary racism'. An untethered signifier in search of a use, this expression agglutinates at least two different meanings: the persecution of believers, which is obviously reprehensible, and the questioning of beliefs, which is practised in all civilized countries. Criticism of a religion falls within the domain of the spirit of examination but certainly not within that of discrimination. Striking a religious believer is a crime. Debating an article of faith, a point of doctrine, is a right. Confusing the two is an intolerable amalgamation.

To put the point still more clearly: insulting a veiled woman in the street, setting fire to, damaging, or looting a mosque, or anathematizing a group of Muslims is tantamount to spitting in the face of the Republic and all its citizens, Christians, Jews, Buddhists, or unbelievers. Although these aggressions must be ruthlessly punished and places of worship protected as part of the national heritage, we must not inhibit or prevent free speech with regard to religious systems. These are two different orders of magnitude. There is already so much real discrimination connected with skin colour, appearance, skills, social status, and accent that it seems pointless to add other forms of discrimination that are fictive or fantastic. Let's imagine that in the eighteenth century the Church had replied to the attacks of Voltaire, Rousseau, Diderot, d'Alembert, and Co. by accusing them of 'racism' (the word did not exist at the time). Let's imagine that the same defence continued down to the twentieth century, and that in response to every challenge to the Bible made by free-thinkers, the ecclesiastical authorities had tried to censure the expression of these arguments by arguing that they constituted the crime of *Christianophobia*. Christianity would have remained frozen, congealed like a phantom vessel, incapable of evolving, of reconsidering its heritage. It was the attacks of its adversaries that regenerated it, awakened it from its long dogmatic slumber.

Let's face it: the undertaking conducted here may be doomed in advance. The expression 'Islamophobia' has entered the global lexicon. It has become a juridical, political shield that makes it possible to ward off all criticisms, but that is not a reason for giving up. Languages sometimes fall ill, as we have seen in the history of totalitarianism in the twentieth century. To borrow an expression from Camus, which is repeated *ad nauseam*: 'calling things by the wrong name adds to the affliction of the world'. The battle is first of all philosophical: anyone who expropriates words, expropriates brains and places mendacity at the heart of language. For the time being, the fundamentalists have won the vocabulary battle, but there is still time to stop this excessively well-oiled machine. Delegitimizing the term 'Islamophobia', instilling doubt about it, putting it permanently between quotation marks – that is the goal of this essay. To win the war against fundamentalism, we have to fight it first on the terrain of ideas. Here I offer a small toolbox for deconstructing the witch-hunt and rejecting the blackmail.

Part I

The Fabrication of a Crime of Opinion

1

The Disappearance of Race, the Proliferation of Racists

Écr.l'inf., abbreviation of 'Écrasons l'infâme' (i.e., 'let us crush obscurantism and superstition'): Voltaire's signature at the end of his letters.

On 16 May 2013, the French parliament, acting on a proposal made by the Front de gauche, decided to eliminate the notion of 'race' from legislation, 'in order to move our society forward on the ideological and pedagogical level, even though we are all convinced that this symbolic gesture will not suffice to do away with racism' (François Ascensi).[1] During his campaign, the presidential candidate (François Hollande) had in fact supported this move, in order to cut the ground from under 'all the nauseating theories'. The delegate who presented the proposal, Alfred Marie-Jeanne,[2] emphasized that the word 'race' is an 'aberrant concept'. Having served as the basis for the worst excesses, 'it has no place in our juridical order'. Already taboo in common discourse, the term has more or less fallen into disuse, except in far-right homilies and in rap songs. The initiative is revelatory of our desire to resolve problems by nullifying them. If there are no longer any races, then the word 'racism' ought to disappear. There are no longer any races except the proliferating race of racists, who are proliferating like vermin in need of re-education. To eliminate these differences, we have to stress one difference that cannot be overcome, that of the racist, who is cast out into the absolute otherness of the barbarian. Thus all we have to do is cut out the tumour, eradicate the accursed word, and everything will be fine.

The approval of this law occurred in the context of a new wave of hostile acts among citizens of various groups, and thus of a tendency the inverse of that proclaimed by the elites. In the schools, in the street, in the media, and in song lyrics, the fine drama of unanimity disintegrated into insults, fights, and diverse abusive epithets such as 'feujs' (Jews), 'rebeus' (Arabs), 'gaulois' (Gauls), 'céfrans' (French), 'noiches' (Asians), and many more. The hymn sung to happy coexistence corresponds to the image of a fragmented humanity. We have never shouted so much at people in the name of their origins, their beliefs, or the colour of their skin. In a movement already noted by those most lucid observers, Paul Yonnet and Pierre-André Taguieff, anti-racism never ceases to racialize every form of ethnic, political, sexual, or religious conflict. It constantly recreates the curse that it claims to be fighting. A strange mechanism whose genealogy should be traced; it is probably connected with the collapse of the communist project. Everywhere, racial struggle seems to be supplanting class struggle, as Raymond Aron already feared sixty years ago.[3] Everything has become racial: cultures, religions, communities, sexual preferences, thoughts, eating habits. Hasn't the neologism 'pauvrophobie' ('pauperphobia') recently been invented (ATD Quart monde, October 2016) to denounce discriminations in job insecurity? A purely linguistic poultice that will in no way improve the situation of those excluded, but that reassures social actors. With this strange contradiction that assimilates fear to hatred, 'phobias' are proliferating. To fear a group, a gender orientation, a belief, or a working-class accent is already to display loathing, to oscillate between aversion and mental illness. The phobic person is twice guilty, on both the psychic and the social levels. We haven't nullified the problem, we've just moved it. Everything that distinguishes humans ends up setting them against one another. The slightest disagreement or uneasiness is translated into a racial disqualification: as soon as one person feels attacked, even by a look or an expression, he can accuse you, point an avenging finger at you.

What should an anti-racism, rightly understood, consist in? The wisdom to live together, the attraction of diversity when individuals of all origins encounter one another in the same space, but also a discerning intelligence capable of distinguishing what is a matter of humiliation from what is a matter of freedom of expression. Let us recall that the goal of a wise politics is to prevent discord and avoid war. But anti-racism, which has become the civil religion of modern times, has been transformed into a permanent war of all against all, a rhetoric of recrimination. The contraction of time and space brought about by new technologies and means of transportation leads to the abolition of the distances that used to protect us from what was far away. But on a planet where human tribes, constantly on the move, collide with one another, the pressure becomes oppressive. The net tightens, arousing a feeling of claustrophobia and even of rejection. Globalization reflects this historical moment, at which the Earth becomes aware of its limits and humans become aware of their interdependence. The universe ceases to be the common space of their intercourse and becomes the site of their mutual torments. Since people are now separated from each other by no more than a few hours in an airplane or a train, they are deprived of the distance required by any relationship and plunged into the intolerable proximity of the global village, precisely where distances, intervals, need to be re-established so that everyone rediscovers his place. The opening-up promised by modernity, the marvellous possibility of leaving behind the local, the native, the tribal, is converted into a new confinement on the global scale, not so much a broadening of horizons as the perception of the horizon as a new enclosure. Since there is only one world, that of population explosions, natural catastrophes, and mass migrations, it is more necessary than ever that people conceive of themselves as large groups. Tensions increase because individuals come closer to one another, rub shoulders, are forced to share space. To build bridges between people, you have to start by restoring the gates that delimit each person's territory.

Finally, the dominant 'racism', that disease of world unification, is no longer connected solely with a wish to exterminate, as it was in Germany, Turkey, Cambodia, or Rwanda; it is above all a desire to confine. It expresses the desire to be among one's own kind and to drive out intruders: the danger facing multiracial societies is as much the dictatorship of a majority that imposes its law as it is the juxtaposition of communities hermetically sealed off from one another, communicating no more than the strict minimum. In this configuration, everything that distinguishes people ends up wounding them. So sensitivities have to be handled with extreme care, and one has to think twice before saying anything at all. Any offensive remark, class contempt, comment on physical appearance, or even a compliment can be interpreted as discrimination. All that remains is humour, which mitigates clichés and routs them, whereas racist jokes confirm them by making people laugh at the expense of this or that category of others.

A major change in modern times: in Western

countries, the politics of identity is tending to replace help for the disadvantaged. The People, as presented mythically by the left and the republicans, is disappearing in favour of minorities. Everywhere, the ethnic is supplanting the social, the ethical is supplanting the political, and living memory is supplanting cold history. Everywhere the loathsome habit of defining oneself by one's origins, identity, or belief is settling in. Difference is reaffirmed at the very time that we want to establish equality, at the risk of involuntarily continuing the old prejudices connected with skin colour and customs. This tendency is contemporary with the explosion of the judicial in the modern world. The courtroom is becoming the site where reparations compensate victims and nail to the pillory the villains who have dared to cross the line. If in the democratic age the court trial has become the pedagogical trope par excellence, that is because it is where everyone defends the most cherished cause of all, oneself, and displays before witnesses one's suffering and one's humiliations. The trio of the attorney, the judge, and the plaintiff consecrates the court as the emblematic stage on which the human adventure is played out in the age of identity.

As for the critique of political correctness (a euphemism that has been raised to the rank of an *art de vivre*), it is itself another kind of conformism, a convention of the unconventional, an orthodoxy of heterodoxy that merely doubles one dead-end by adding another. We're not going to insult one another to show our freedom of opinion. The fact that we have to restrain ourselves in making judgements regarding those close to us is not a simple matter of censorship but the minimal decency that we owe each other in pluralistic societies. Politeness, as Kant already pointed out, is politics writ small. If a Donald Trump could be elected president of the United States, it is because in the course of his campaign he ignored this elementary courtesy, insulting Mexicans, immigrants, blacks, Muslims, Chinese, and indeed anyone who objected to his programme. But this popular spokesman, who likes to be clownish and Neronian and who defends an isolationist and protectionist credo, is himself no more than the counter-product of American political correctness, to which he replies with the politically direct or even the politically abject. In him, the verbal discipline propagated by the Republican or Democratic elites has as its counterpart impulsive effrontery, insults used as arguments, *ad hominem* attacks, mockery of women and the disabled, death threats against his rivals, a call for the army to practise torture, to commit war crimes... in short, the rhetoric of the mafioso and not that of a responsible politician.

What is political correctness? An allergy to naming things, a sweeping-away of difficulties, the impossibility of saying anything without using metaphor, displacement, gibberish. Words are blurred the way genitals are blurred on some statues, and as piano legs, according to popular legend, were skirted in the Victorian period to avoid offending polite society. Saying what is the case, saying what one sees, would be shocking. Now 'to stigmatize' is to mention that which must not be mentioned. We 'stigmatize' as soon as we point to a problem. Let us recall that during their respective terms as president, both Barack Obama and François Hollande seemed incapable of speaking of 'Islamic terrorism' or 'radical Islam', instead always using indirect or neutral expressions to describe our enemies. The contemporary taboo seeks to shelter not only beliefs or ideas, but whole areas of reality. In certain American universities, for example, students have protested the mere use of the term 'Islamism' or 'radical Islam', regarding it as inappropriate.[4]

In our multiracial and multicultural societies, insulting

minorities is prohibited by law. And that represents progress. It is one of the taboos that constitute what we are. Since 1945, the overt expression of racism, what in English is called 'hate speech', has been connected with an intention to commit murder. The fact that people are no longer allowed to proclaim loud and clear on television or in public that Jews, Arabs, blacks, North Africans, whites, Catholics, or Muslims should be killed is in itself a good thing. The counterpart of this progress: to avoid being accused of racism, one has to proceed with kid gloves, resort to neutral expressions that lead to neither reproach nor prosecution. A kind of lexical decorum weighs on our speech. Describing a person, a minority, or a religion requires an acute sense of nuances. Metaphors that say one thing for another proliferate, and presuppose that everyone will be able to decipher them. But to extend this prudence to the products of human culture, to ban *a priori* any criticism of a system, of a religion, is to risk amputating freedom of thought. That risk was taken in France by the Pleven law of 1972, which created a new crime of 'provoking discrimination, hatred, or violence' committed against individuals 'because of their membership or non-membership in a specific ethnic group, nation, race, or religion'.[5] The broadening of incrimination to religious convictions provided an opportunity that was seized by fundamentalist, Catholic, and other groups to sue the authors of films they considered defamatory – *Je vous salue, Marie*, by Jean-Luc Godard (1985), *The Last Temptation of Christ*, by Martin Scorsese (1988), and *The People vs. Larry Flynt*, by Miloš Forman (1996). These groups contended, on the grounds that certain words are weapons, 'loaded guns' that can wound (as Jean-Paul Sartre, speaking of collaborationist writers after the war, had already emphasized, citing Brice Parain), that speech mocking or showing contempt for religious faith should be censured. From the death sentence passed on Salman Rushdie for having, according to his accusers, blasphemed against the Prophet in his novel *The Satanic Verses,* to the affair of the cartoons depicting Muhammad that ended with the cold-blooded murder of *Charlie Hebdo*'s whole editorial team on 7 January 2015, there is a fine line between a satirical judgement of other people's beliefs and maximal outrage. It therefore seems that we are faced with a choice between offence and acquiescence. To the delicate question of blasphemy radical Islam adds an important nuance: it kills offenders and does not bother with precautions. Everything that used to be part of the spirit of the Enlightenment – criticism, but also anti-clerical, theological, and philosophical discourse, as well as satire – is now supposed to be seen as defamation.

Finally, the quarrel over Islamophobia is revelatory of another phenomenon: the continual emergence of 'new forms of racism' that are noted with anxious uneasiness. The word 'racism' has acquired a galloping obesity, swallowing up in its definition all sorts of behaviours, attitudes, and rites that had up to this point not been connected with it. Anti-racism, like humanitarianism, is a rapidly expanding market in which each group, in order to exist, has to allege that it has suffered a wound that makes it special. These are no longer associations of citizens who have joined together to combat racism; they are religious or community lobbies that invent new forms of discrimination to justify their existence and receive the maximum of publicity and reparations. Claude Lévi-Strauss already noted this fact: 'nothing so much compromises the struggle against racism, or weakens it from inside, or vitiates it, as the indiscriminating use of the word *racism*, by confusing a false but explicit theory with common inclinations and attitudes from which it would be illusory to imagine that humanity can one day free itself'.[6] A consistent anti-racist is a sleuth who discovers a new form of segregation every morning, delighted to have added this new species to the great taxonomy of progressive thought.

2

A Weapon of Mass Intimidation

> Everything has to be taken literally in the Quran: we
> don't engage in commentary because it is a field beyond
> the reach of our reason.
>
> Tarek Obrou, then a member of the Muslim
> Brotherhood, in a lecture given in the 1990s.[1]

Before going any further, let us recall a fundamental
difference between the British Empire and the French
Empire: whereas the latter was motivated by the
conviction that it was bringing freedom and civilization
to countries overseas ('It is the duty of the superior
races to civilize the inferior races', Jules Ferry said in
a famous speech to the Chamber of Deputies in 1885),
the former appears to have had no ambition other
than the extension of trade and profits. It was content
to exploit the riches of distant lands – sometimes via
'indirect rule', but if need be by force – leaving to the
natives the task of administering themselves, while
persisting in their rites and beliefs (modern Great
Britain, multicultural and differentialist, has thus trans-
ferred its imperial model to the home country at the

risk of forgetting the common cement, 'Britishness', and encouraging ethnic separatisms).[2] French imperialism sought to convert Arabs, Africans, and Asians to republican values and to integrate them into the home country, while British imperialism considered Indians, Malays, and Kenyans so different from the British that it deemed vain any attempt to inculcate them into the European way of life. French colonialists claimed to be producing brothers and sisters all over the world, in the name of human rights; conversely, the British respected the diversity of cultures without trying to unify them under a common umbrella. To each his own way of life, no need to change people. Perceived by some as an inferiority or a leftover that could be corrected in time, difference is considered by others to be an unbridgeable gap that there is no point in trying to eliminate. Such is the foundation of communitarian liberalism: the British left their mark on the occupied countries, notably their parliamentary system in India and elsewhere, while the French granted French nationality to their Muslim subjects in Algeria only little by little, contradicting their generous universalist proclamations.

It remains the case that, pushed to its logical extreme, respect for otherness can lead to infamous discriminatory policies: South African apartheid made the Other so distinct from me that he no longer had the right to approach me. Confining everyone in their specificity and forbidding them to move outside it, treating their traditions as sacred, makes it difficult for people to live together, especially in mass societies. Today, the French forbid the Islamic headscarf in schools and the burqa in the public sphere because they consider all people equal; Britons put individuals in a hierarchy and connect them with their community. That is the ambivalence of anti-racism: it defends humanity as a single family, but sees in cultural diversities so many small homelands to be protected in spite of everything. A given minority's almost neurotic concern to avoid any impure contact, to persist in its mores, is warmly supported, but our encouragement to resist contradicts the advice that we give it. We make overtures to this minority even as it withdraws from us, we construct new bridges even as it takes pride in burning the old ones, we celebrate in it what we criticize in ourselves, the inveterate ethnocentrism. Then we risk, as a whole section of the far left does, being slower to grant Muslims the rights we enjoy – for example, the right not to practise a religion or to practise it intermittently. The celebration of diversity as a supreme norm can in no case provide a common foundation. It is the very idea of human equality that is abandoned. Here is a proof, if ever there was one, that unreserved praise of cultural particularities can also conceal a neo-colonial paternalism: in October 2013, in Istanbul, the Organization of Islamic Cooperation, which is financed by dozens of Muslim countries that shamelessly persecute Jews, Hindus, Buddhists, and Christians, asked Western nations – incarnated by the US Secretary of State, Hillary Clinton, and the European Union's High Representative for foreign affairs and security policy, Catherine Ashton – to put an end to freedom of expression, at least in so far as Islam is concerned, claiming that Islam is represented too negatively as a religion that oppresses women and proselytizes aggressively. The petitioners wanted to make criticism of Islam, and notably the identification of Muslims with terrorists, an international crime recognized by the highest authorities. Every year since 1999, the fifty-seven countries of the Organization of Islamic Cooperation have sought to establish a crime of blasphemy before the UN's Human Rights Commission (replaced by the United Nations Human Rights Council in 2006). Formulated at the World Conference on Racism held in Durban, South Africa, in 2001, this demand has been repeated almost every year in the various international authorities. For example, in September 2007 the UN special reporter on racism, Doudou Diène, a Senegalese jurist, presented a report to the Human Rights Council in which he described Islamophobia as one 'of the most serious forms taken by the defamation of religions'. In March of the same year, the Human Rights Council compared this type of 'defamation' to racism pure and simple and demanded that any mockery of the Prophet and Islamic symbols be forbidden.

Thus there was a twofold ambition: to shut up Westerners, who were guilty of three mortal sins – freedom of religion, freedom of thought, and the equality of men and women – but especially to create an instrument for the internal policing of reformist or liberal Muslims who dared to criticize their religion and who called for changes in family law, parity between the sexes, the right to apostasy, conversion, or even the possibility of 'de-fasting' (*dé-jeuner*; in France, Morocco, and Algeria there are Muslims who decide to cease participating in the Ramadan fast for personal reasons, but encounter the hostility of those close to them or even of the authorities, and eat in secret; it is estimated that about a third of the 5 or 6 million Muslims in France do not observe Ramadan).[3] Thus Muslims who demand the option of being intermittent believers, like many Christians and Jews, have to be condemned. These renegades must be exposed to public vilification by their fellow Muslims and said to be imbued with colonial ideology, in order to block any hope of a change in the Land of Islam. And this must be done with the unctuousness of the useful idiots of the left or the far left, who are always on the lookout for a new racism, and who are certain that they have found in Islam the last oppressed subject of History. We used to point to those who contested that view: Salman Rushdie, Ayaan Hirsi Ali, Taslima Nasreen,

Irshad Manji; today, we point to Chahdortt Djavann, Malika Sorel, Dounia Bouzar, Kamel Daoud, Waleed al-Husseini, and Boualem Sansal. For example, in February 2016 a collective of historians and academics sent to the Paris daily newspaper *Le Monde* a petition accusing the Algerian writer Kamel Daoud of peddling Islamophobic stereotypes in his interpretation of the events in Cologne on New Year's Eve 2015 (when more than 500 German women were the victims of sexual aggression by young men, mostly from North Africa).[4] In an op-ed published on 31 January 2016, Daoud noted the pathological relation between the attitudes to sexuality in many Islamic countries and the cultural shock felt by some people from North Africa upon encountering women walking freely through the streets. Daoud was not the first to make this diagnosis – from Chahdortt Djavann, Irshad Manji, Wafa Sultan, and Ayaan Hirsi Ali to Tahar Ben Jelloun and Fethi Benslama, many writers, political scientists, novelists, and psychoanalysts, themselves natives of the Middle East or North Africa, have drawn attention to women's sexual dissatisfaction and banishment, and to the prohibition on homosexuality, in the Arab Muslim world – but he made the mistake of applying this analysis to the events that had just occurred in Cologne. For the signatories of the petition, the goal was not to express their disagreement or to qualify the Algerian writer's point of view, but to shut him up by accusing him of racism, while he was the object of a *fatwa* issued by a Salafist imam in Algeria in 2015 that called for his execution.[5] With this petition, we are no longer in the domain of legitimate intellectual debate, but in that of demonology. The authors of the petition suggest that the events that occurred in Cologne are so serious that we have to begin by not talking about them. Moreover, they have nothing in particular to say about them except that we must not fall 'into the trivialization of racist discourse'; a certain prohibition should weigh on interpretation as soon as it is a matter of people coming from North Africa or the Near East. This represents an incredible reversal characteristic of a whole multicultural 'left': the gospel of anti-racism is more important than the events themselves, respecting cultures is more important than protecting persons. Rape is no longer a crime if it is situated in its context. That is what is explained, for example, by the sociologist Éric Fassin, a specialist in forms of discrimination: 'The task of the social sciences is to be wary of essentialist explanations. It is not because these people are Muslims that they have committed these acts. There is a political purpose. Whom did they attack? White German women. They didn't go to rape prostitutes. That gives a meaning to their violence.'[6] In other words, sexual aggression toward white, therefore 'dominant', women has a meaning that attenuates or minimizes the import of the crime, which becomes a political act. As a result, the horror of rape is diluted in the broader saga of the emancipation of the wretched of the Earth.

So woe be to liberal Muslims who dare to criticize their religion or question their countries' mores. The religious police cracks down on these ethnic renegades, these deserters whose efforts to express themselves must be nipped in the bud. Thus another expert on Islam, Alain Gresh, a journalist with *Le Monde diplomatique*, took the liberty, during a hearing in the Senate on 10 February 2016, of discrediting the imam of Drancy, Hassan Chalghoumi, whose principal crime was to have visited Israel and not been hostile to Jews: 'The imam Chalghoumi, who is idolized by the media, is not taken seriously in the Muslim community. Muslims consider his performance an insult.'[7] Let us recall that the imam of Drancy, having been condemned to death by the fundamentalists, still lives surrounded by bodyguards. As for French Muslim intellectuals and liberal journalists, such as Abdennour Bidar, Abdelwahab Meddeb (who died in 2016), Waleed al-Husseini (a Palestinian who took refuge in France), Mohamed Sifaoui, and Malek Chebel, an Algerian historian, they are 'turncoat media hounds' (*repentis médiatiques*) who justify non-Muslims' visceral Islamophobia.[8] What about the feminists of Ni Putes ni Soumises,[9] for example? They are far-right activists contaminated by their alliance with identitarian movements.[10] They are all 'native auxiliaries', Pierre Tevanian claims, speaking of people like their spokesperson at the time, Sihem Habchi.[11] Or else, as a member of Indigènes de la République (Natives of the Republic, a small identitarian religious group), they are 'auxiliaries of the racist system' whose task is to 'finish off the contemptible North African family'.[12] The expression is interesting, signifying two complementary things: that a female French citizen of North African origin nonetheless remains North African, such that she can never become a full-fledged French citizen. And that a Muslim woman remains a Muslim woman forever, a prisoner of her culture of origin. It is strange to see how much a certain leftism peddles these extremely threadbare colonial clichés.

What we are witnessing is thus truly a witch-hunt, conducted by the fundamentalists and their Marxist-influenced allies, who have formed a coalition to keep Islam united and immovable. Any hope of change in the Land of Islam has to be blocked, and dissidents have to be attacked.

The accusation of being Islamophobic is nothing other than a weapon of mass destruction in intellectual debate. For the past twenty years we have been witnessing the fabrication of a new crime of opinion, analogous to what used to be done in the Soviet Union to silence 'enemies of the people'. The guardians of dogma keep a wary eye out for the slightest transgression or allusion. Simply mentioning a 'Muslim problem' will call down the anathema of the censors and threats to sue.[13] Thus the goal is to denigrate the young women who want to take off the veil and walk bareheaded on the street without being constantly insulted, who want to marry those they love and not those who are imposed on them; to strike down these French, English, Germans, and Italians of Turkish, Pakistani, Algerian, and African origin who are demanding the right to be indifferent to religion and who want to live their lives without obligatory allegiance to their native community. The question is shifted from the intellectual level to the cultural level, every objection or desire to secede being seen as a 'racist' betrayal. The qualifier is strange because, classically, racism consists in seeing in skin colour, ethnic group, or the clan an insurmountable determinism. But now the attempt to escape from it is itself denounced as a racist act.

The anathema also affects the academic world, as is proven by the quarrel that arose in 2008 between the medievalist Alain de Libera, a professor at the prestigious Collège de France, and the historian Sylvain Gouguenheim, who was called an 'erudite Islamophobe' for having maintained that the role of Arabs in the transmission of ancient knowledge was marginal.[14] What should have remained a respectable disagreement limited to the level of scholarship – it is difficult for a non-specialist to judge the issues involved – was transformed into a witch-hunt. Sylvain Gouguenheim was accused of coming from the far right and minimizing the role of Muslims in the construction of intellectual Europe. Whereas the medievalist Jacques Le Goff judged Gouguenheim's book 'interesting but debatable', and deplored the vehemence of the polemics, the philosopher Alain de Libera, assuming the role of Grand Inquisitor, lumped together under the rubric of Islamophobia not only Sylvain Gouguenheim but also Fernand Braudel, Pope Benedict XVI, Rémi Brague, and Marie-Thérèse and Dominique Urvoy, all of them deemed guilty of sacrificing to 'identitarian monoliths'. When a scholar sinks into polemics and starts putting things on the Index, he does not escape the facile arguments he attributes to others.

3

The Miracle of
Transubstantiation

The great religions are lucrative agencies for travel to
the beyond. But no one has ever come back to tell us
whether the journey was worth the trouble.

Søren Kierkegaard

A mystery remains: that of the transformation of
religion into race, since the racialization of the world
seems to be the most tangible result of the battle against
discrimination over the past century. As we know, a
major religion like Islam or Christianity includes a
relatively varied group of peoples across four continents, and cannot be assimilated to a particular ethnic
group. To speak of Islamophobia is thus to keep alive
the confusion between a system of beliefs and the
faithful who adhere to it. Criticizing Islam or attacking
it as a system is said to amount to denigrating Muslims
(who do not necessarily identify with their religion),
and mocking Christian dogmas is said to amount to
denigrating all Christians. Thus Rabelais, Erasmus,
Voltaire, Diderot, and Rousseau are supposed not
merely to have impugned the Church's dogmas but to

have trampled on the faith of millions of believers who should have nailed them to the pillory for their offence. Similarly, to mock atheism or challenge scepticism is to trample on all atheists, and to mock agnostics is to 'stigmatize' them. But contesting a belief, rejecting principles one considers absurd or false, is the very basis of intellectual and even religious life, because religions, just like ideologies, have a date of birth: must we speak of capitalistophobia, liberalophobia, socialismophobia, and communistophobia?

In a civilized system, we have the right to reject the great religions as a whole, to consider them puerile, retrograde, stultifying. We have the right to call Moses, Jesus, and Muhammad the 'Three Imposters', according to the famous thesis that has been known in Europe ever since the thirteenth century, and that Louis Massignon traces back to a sect of dissident Ismailites in the kingdom of Bahrain in the tenth century. Their sovereign, Abu Tahir Sulayman (907–44), is supposed to have written: 'In this world, three individuals have corrupted people: a shepherd, a physician, and a camel-driver. And this camel-driver was the worst conjuror, the worst swindler of the three.' For those who do not believe, religions are merely fictions, more or less fantastic or absurd stories. People who consider them from a distance or with incredulity should not be punished by being cast into dungeons or, worse yet, by terrorism, that random inquisition. The fact that a writer like Michel Houellebecq could have been taken to court by the Paris Mosque for having said, in 2001, 'The stupidest religion is after all Islam. When one reads the Quran, one is crushed, just crushed', tells us a great deal about the regressive condition we are in.[1] Saying the same about Judaism, Christianity, or Buddhism would hardly have raised an eyebrow. The only thing that is forbidden is persecuting believers or hindering the exercise of a religion, provided that it also respects the laws in force. A flagrant counter-example: even though Christian minorities in Syria, Turkey, Sudan, Niger, and Pakistan are persecuted, killed, exterminated, or driven to flee the country, even though in Europe cathedrals, basilicas, and churches are placed under police protection and believers are threatened, the word 'Christianophobia', suggested by the UN's reporters, is not used and never will be.

A strange blindness: formerly across most of the Near East and North Africa, Christianity was wiped out by the rapid Arab conquest that invaded Spain and Portugal, launched incursions into France, and landed in Italy (in 846, Rome was sacked by Arab Muslim armies reinforced by Berber converts).[2] These days, at least in the Near East, Africa, and Central Asia, Christianity is the religion of the martyr: in Syria before the civil war, there were some 2 million Christians protected by Bashar al-Assad. Forty per cent of them had to emigrate, driven into exile by the 'moderate' Syrian opposition, the al-Nusra Front or ISIL. In 1987 there were 1.4 million Christians in Iraq. After the two Gulf Wars, there remain hardly 400,000.[3] In Egypt, the Copts, though protected by the government, are regularly murdered, kidnapped, persecuted. In Niamey and Zinder, in Niger, on 16 and 17 January 2015, in response to a new cover of *Charlie* considered defamatory, protesters burned forty-five Christian churches, a school, an orphanage, and a cultural centre in riots that resulted in ten deaths and almost 200 wounded. In France, a country with an anti-clerical tradition, one can make fun of Moses, Jesus, the Dalai Lama, or the pope, represent them in every posture, even the most grotesque or obscene, but one is never allowed to laugh at Islam, on pain of incurring the wrath of the law courts or execution by jihadist vigilantes. Islam and Islam alone, of all the great religions, is supposed to be spared disapproval and mockery.

What is the reason for this preferential treatment? It is that transubstantiation, or the transformation of one substance into another, is a kind of magic. First, a pariah image has to be constructed. For example, it is undeniable that Muslims are oppressed in Myanmar, but they are oppressed mainly by other Muslims – Shias, Sunnis, or radicals. If there are massacres, most of them involve Muslims killing Muslims. We must not 'essentialize' Islam, we are told over and over, unless it is to make it a victim and a saviour. To arrive at this result, people do not hesitate to resort to all sorts of pious imagery, used in other times with regard to Maoism or Stalinism. Like the proletariat according to Marxism, Muslims are supposed to be the salt of the earth. A truly human person can only be Muslim. Do you want proof of this? According to the philosopher Pierre Tevanian, all 'whites' are racists, and all Muslims are spontaneously progressives: 'it is just as established statistically that racist, xenophobic, and Islamophobic opinions are more widespread among whites than among non-whites'.[4] A fine example of essentialism: the whiteness of people's skin is supposed to dispose them spontaneously to racism (so that we can only congratulate the author of this quotation on having escaped that biological fatality). A little further on, Tevanian writes: 'The panels of Muslims polled are distinctly more progressive than the rest of the population on questions such as social welfare, the redistribution of wealth, racism, and xenophobia.'[5] Apart from the eminently fantastic invocation of statistics, let us note that this moral superiority is purely arbitrary.

Why is this religion chosen to the exclusion of all others? Because it is the substitute for a moribund Marxism and Third-Worldism,[6] because it embodies a power of devotion that has left us. Hence Islam and its believers must be treated with a kind of tact, patience, and adroitness that neither Jews nor Christians, nor

Buddhists nor Hindus, require. Thus, as Régis Debray explains, we have to distinguish opinions, which are revocable and fragile, from convictions, which involve the whole being. Convictions, even if they cannot claim the status of universal truths, constitute 'a living centre of life, of sharing and influence'.[7] Debray concludes: 'An opinion can be contradicted; a conviction is wounded or slammed.' But democratic maturity presupposes that I accept the fact that, for others, my most intimate convictions and my certainty that I am in possession of the truth are mere opinions. If I want to convince them that my certainties are well founded, I have to use the weapon of argumentation, of persuasion, of dialectic, and not that of the dagger or the revolver. If others' beliefs could never be challenged, humanity would never have emerged from blind faith and would have maintained the primitive forms of religion. All monotheisms arose by moving beyond pagan or polytheistic rites, whether those of the Greeks, the Romans, the Gauls, the Celts, the Zoroastrians, or the animists. Did anyone ask then whether that wounded the sensitivities of the pontiffs, flamens, druids, shamans, or sorcerers? There comes a time when teaching, the development of mores, and the progress of knowledge may enter into conflict with this or that belief and must in no way bow down before it. Are we going to do away with Darwin's teaching on the grounds that creationists, evangelical Christians, or supporters of Fethullah Gülen oppose it?

But, Debray goes on to ask: don't we shrink back before the Shoah as before a taboo that must not be mocked, whereas we allow Islam to be criticized?[8] Hasn't the Shoah become a new cult before which we bow down? This example, which is classic in the propaganda of the Iranian fundamentalists, conflates two orders that differ in nature: facts and faith, a historical event and a religious belief. It is an epistemological error to put on the same footing a massacre (the Armenian or Tutsi genocides, or the Shoah, all of which can be proven) and a revealed truth, which cannot be proven by reason. If some people dare to criticize Moses, Jesus, Vishnu, Muhammad, or Buddha, then why shouldn't we laugh at Dachau, Bergen-Belsen, or Treblinka, as the ex-president of Iran, Mahmoud Ahmadinejad, did in August 2006 when a competition for caricatures of the Holocaust was organized for the first time in Teheran? A troubling amalgamation: it would occur to no one to make fun of the St Bartholomew's Day massacre, Louis XIV's dragonnades against Protestants, or the killings in the Sabra neighbourhood and the Chatila refugee camp in Lebanon. For some people's certainties not to wound those of others, there must be laws, a habit of living together, common customs compatible with freedom of expression, on the condition that a specific cult does not assume exorbitant rights and does not require special forms of respect denied to others. That's the rub when believers try to encroach on the public space in order to impose their demands – a rejection of swimming lessons and gymnastics for girls, the full-body veil, the 'burkini', etc. It is for the law and not religion to determine what is licit and what is not, and citizens must obey the law, no matter what group they belong to.

A great religion like Islam, which was also an immense civilization, encompasses many different peoples and cannot be identified with a particular ethnic group, even if Arabs are its leading people and its anthropological base. There are as many Islams as there are continents, but they are now becoming more uniform under the yoke of the conquering Wahhabism propagated by Saudi Arabia.[9] The more discrimination concerns persons who are guilty of being what they are – black, Arab, Jewish, yellow, white – the more religious discussion bears on the spirit of the texts, the debatable points that are always subject to exegesis and transformation, because they are themselves the products of a precise history. The racialization of the religious is not a proof of vigour: *religious faith is becoming an identity* that wants to be recognized and protected, and at the same time a group that has a special link with the deity.

Finally, Islam is supposed to deserve special treatment because it is, more than other religions, 'the religion of the oppressed'.[10] This claim seems strange if we consider that some of the richest countries in the world are predominantly Muslim, and that conversely, among the almost 3 billion Christians, there are hundreds of millions of underprivileged and outcast people. A religion is not judged positively or negatively depending on the living standard of the individuals that are presumed to practise it or on the nature of the political system where it is predominant. It is true that most Arab Muslim states are despotic – with a few exceptions, including Tunisia – but that only makes a critique of the religious foundation of these same governments even more urgent. Furthermore, in France a whole middle class of North African origin has emerged over the past half-century, and to flourish it has no need of Emmanuel Todd's compassion. But to speak of oppression is to connect the Prophet's faith to the whole phraseology of the 'wretched of the Earth' peculiar to the left, and it is to grant that phraseology a final reprieve. What is improperly called 'Arab Muslim humiliation' is first of all the fact that many societies that do not follow the Quran's teachings (China, Russia, Southeast Asia, the United States, Europe, Latin America) are more successful economically and politically, and also that in the end a large part of the globe has no interest in Islam. More than hostility, it is the observation of this indifference that is humiliating, just as the mere existence of other religions that confront Islam with the shock of their unbearable alterity is experienced as an insult. How can the best of all revelations, that of the Prophet, be ignored by infidels, non-believers, or, worse yet, atheists? Islamophobia is first of all the name of a narcissistic wound that has been inverted into resentment.

Part II

The Left Suffering from Denial

For a modern Western mind, it is inconceivable that people might fight and die in such great numbers for simple religious differences [...] we cannot accept the idea that a whole civilization might, in matters of loyalty, accord primacy to religion [...]. An attitude that is reflected in the current inability, as political as much as it is journalistic and scientific, to recognize the importance of the religious factor in current affairs in the Muslim world; and in the consequent recourse to a language that depends on the notions of left and right, of progressives and conservatives, on a whole Western terminology whose use, for the purpose of explaining the Muslim political phenomenon, is about as appropriate and enlightening as an account of a tennis match given by a specialist in rugby.

Bernard Lewis[1]

4

Islamo-Leftism, or the Conjunction of Resentments

> If one were looking for a barrack-room religion, Islam would seem to be the ideal solution: strict observance of rules [...], detailed inspections and meticulous cleanliness (ritual ablutions), masculine promiscuity both in spiritual matters and in the carrying out of the organic functions; and no women.
>
> Claude Lévi-Strauss, *Tristes Tropiques*[2]

In 1994, Chris Harman, the leader of the Socialist Workers' Party, the minuscule British political party affiliated with the Fourth International, published a long article entitled 'The Prophet and the Proletariat'.[3] In it he advocated an alliance between left-wing activists and radical Muslim groups that he thought it would be wrong to describe as retrograde. On the contrary, he maintained, we should return these lost sheep of Islam to the fold of the left, and mobilize them in the service of the only cause that matters – the destruction of capitalism:

> The left has made two mistakes in relation to the
> Islamists in the past. The first has been to write them
> off as fascists, with whom we have nothing in common.
> The second has been to see them as 'progressives' who
> must not be criticised. These mistakes have jointly
> played a part in helping the Islamists to grow at the
> expense of the left in much of the Middle East. The
> need is for a different approach that sees Islamism as the
> product of a deep social crisis which it can do nothing
> to resolve, and which fights to win some of the young
> people who support it to a very different, independent,
> revolutionary socialist perspective.

Pointing out that only the rich are required to pay the
Islamic tax, the 2.5 per cent levy to help poor people,
Harman saw in the call for the return of the caliphate,
to the practices of the age of the Prophet, a way of
revolting against the situation of the period. The goal is
to revive the founding spirit of Islam as Khomeini did
in his time. The fundamentalists, Harman argues, don't
want to return to the past so much as to merge tradition
and modernity by regenerating religion. Therefore, not
all of them are reactionaries. He explains that Islamism
is a revolutionary movement that is the vehicle of real
class interests, but he does not follow his logic all the
way to its end. Certain classes, notably in agriculture,
have lost the comfort of their earlier way of life
without gaining any kind of economic security. The
mosque then becomes their landmark, a transitional
point between a poorly understood modernity and a
traditional environment. But these politico-religious
movements are not really progressive: they stop short
of threatening the petty bourgeoisie, and while they
mobilize popular anger, they also smother it. In matters
of religion, according to a paradox already noticed
by Marx, it is difficult to distinguish resistance from
oppression. Hence in the Land of Islam, uprisings often
degenerate into fratricidal battles. Islamists are able to

crystallize the majority's anger and follow 'the orders of a secret central committee', but they go only halfway. Their radicalism is a utopia emanating from a section of the new petty bourgeoisie whose social status has declined. We can neither condemn nor approve them in their repression of free women, homosexuals, and ethnic or religious minorities. Harman's conclusion: 'The Islamists are not our allies. [...] But this does not mean we can simply take an abstentionist, dismissive attitude to [them].' Revolutionary concepts must therefore take advantage of these contradictions. 'Where the Islamists are in opposition, our rule should be, "with the Islamists sometimes, with the state never".'

The irony of this analysis consists entirely in its disproportion: it came from a microscopic sect, formed by dissidents in a dying communist movement, considering whether it was opportune or not to ally itself to a religion with a billion and a half believers. Islam speaks in the name of God, Chris Harman speaks in the name of Leon Trotsky – that aborted Stalin, the radical loser of Bolshevism, assassinated in Mexico in 1940 by Ramón Mercader, on the orders of the 'little father of the peoples'. Whence the imbalance of the Socialist Workers' Party: this small group with a few thousand activists, a product of the Fourth International's multiple schisms, demands the right to criticize religion, the right to practise it. It demands the right not to wear the veil or the right to wear it 'in racist countries like France', not only for speakers of Arabic in Algeria, but also for speakers of Berber and of French. The result is a political hotchpotch that seeks to reconcile contraries and proves the difficulty of combining the most intransigent Marxism with theologico-political considerations. Thus it is a question of enlisting the Islamists in the old new left, of performing a feat of political acrobatics. But these 'leftists of Allah' (Claude Askolovitch) are not much concerned about being consistent. They will adopt the strategy characteristic of the Trotskyists, 'entryism': infiltrating the Islamist movement in order to take advantage of its energy while at the same time diverting it from its goal. A risky strategy that might be turned against them. The hope nourished by a minority fringe of the far left that it can make use of radical Islam as the spearhead of a new insurrection is not without ulterior motives on both sides: radical Islam also dreams of infiltrating the battalions of the progressive camp in order to advance its pawns under cover of this moral sanction. At the very least, it is a pact between dupes. A twofold deception, apparently: one side supports wearing the veil in Europe in the name of the battle against Islamophobia and state racism. The other borrows a revolutionary rhetoric, pretending to attack the market and globalization the better to impose the spread of the Quranic faith. The far left is certain that there is no religious fanaticism because religion is not autonomous: there is only 'the rage of capitalism's victims'. Everything is reduced to a common denominator: the economy. Islam itself is a mere phantasmagoria. As Alain Badiou puts it, 'our problem comes from farther back',[4] from the historical failure of communism, which set free capitalism's bestial energy. And in this void, a suicidal nihilism borrows the paths of religion like a 'hallucination', for lack of a global strategic proposal for young people. To believe Badiou, the jihadists and suicide bombers are upset chiefly about the fall of the Berlin Wall![5] The far left is sure that *radical Islam has chosen the wrong kind of radicalness*. Its misguided energy gets lost in dogma instead of attacking the mercantile monster.

But these common bonds against the same enemy (big capital) are not merely opportunistic. Beyond leftism and devotion, both camps share the same experience: that of being relegated to the ashcan of history. The communist dream collapsed in 1989, just as Islam fell into decadence centuries ago, and still more after 1924, when Ataturk, determined to establish a secular state in Turkey, abolished the caliphate. Islam, 'disconsolate at its destitution',[6] is a wounded religion that dreams of restoring its lost grandeur. The systematic recourse to terrorism is a proof not of vitality but of panic. Ultraviolence is a symptom of impotence. If the far left courts totalitarian theocracies as it courted one-party dictatorships, *it is also out of solidarity with other losers*: it is taking revenge for its setbacks by associating itself with the only force capable of worrying the Western world, Islamic radicalism. It is a conjunction of resentments, a grouping of the afflicted. The left has lost everything – the working class, the USSR, China, Cambodia, the Third World – with the exception of Islam, the new International of the outcasts. The neo-Bolshevist bigotry of the lost believers in Marxism is touching in so far as it forces activists to make the most painful ideological contortions. Islam becomes the last great narrative to which they can cling and which replaces communism, decolonization, and pan-Arabism. In the category of the good revolutionary subject, the Mujahideen, the Fedayeen, the Jihadists, and the martyrs of Hamas or al-Qaeda replace the proletarian, the guerrillero, the wretched of the Earth, the Palestinian. The revolution, that great absence, is now borne by the faithful of the Crescent. The grandeur and dignity of Muslims comes from the fact that they and they alone are now the Bearers of the Promise.

But the far left no longer wants power, just the power to do harm. It seeks to convert its theoretical, political, and philosophical impotence into a power to obstruct, to prevent. Its new love for Islam is just a detour taken the better to attack its immemorial adversary, Capital and the West. To say that one is 'for the Muslims'[7] is simply to brandish a different stick with which to beat bourgeois society, since one cannot destroy it.

This transition took place when the Shah of Iran was overthrown in 1979, an event that truly constituted the matrix of our blindnesses. It was Michel Foucault who started things off with his usual brio. In his enthusiasm, he went to Iran; never having been a Marxist, he didn't care a fig about failed revolutions, 1848, the Paris Commune, Cuba, Beijing, Phnom Penh. He was looking for a new thrill, a spiritual subversion that would make the classical anti-colonialist schemas obsolete. No more laborious professions of faith regarding class struggle or the battle against imperialism. Belief mobilizes the masses better than the naive hope for the advent of socialism: having just read Henry Corbin, a great specialist on Shiism, Foucault saw in Teheran the resurrection, in the middle of the Orient, of Savonarola's or Thomas Munzer's sermons – in short, the emergence of a 'political spirituality'. It was for him 'the insurrection of bare-handed men who want to raise the terrible burden that weighs on each of us but especially on them, these oil workers, these peasants on the borders of empires: the weight of the whole world. It is perhaps the first great insurrection against planet-wide systems, the most modern and the maddest form of revolt.' It was these fanatics rising up against the Shah's regime and the Western world who incarnated the hope for justice and bore in themselves a messianic potential beyond frontiers and countries. In Teheran, Marx's opium of the people had become the indispensable *viaticum* of renewal. The Iranians wanted not only to change their ruler but also 'to change themselves [...] to renew their whole lives by reconnecting with a spiritual experience that they thought they had found at the very heart of Shiite Islam'.[8] Religion was the bearer of a radical demand for the transformation of the self.

In the end, preferring 'the enigma of the uprising' to anti-capitalist revolution, Foucault saw his hopes dashed by the regime's development. Despite his redoubtable lucidity and his will to invent a 'transcendental journalism', he succumbed to the exoticism of the oriental saviour. In a text full of subtle distinctions and difficulties, he explained that uprising is inherent in human societies, even if it leads to a new form of tyranny. But the latter does not nullify the former's vivifying force.[9] Clearly, Michel Foucault was a little short of the anti-totalitarian wisdom that was being shown by dissidents in the communist world at the time. A prisoner of his earplugs, he succumbed to the anti-Western prejudices that characterized the intellectual elite. He forgot that in the twentieth century revolt lost its innocence. It no longer grounds its own legitimacy, it no longer has every right: it has to justify, as it unfolds, the universe it announces; it has to prove that it is not moved by a dreadful desire for revenge. It may always be right to revolt, as people said in 1968, but rebels are not always right about everything. In this regard, it would have sufficed to read Ayatollah Khomeini's very clear writings about his hatred of parliamentary democracy and Western civilization.[10]

In a more classic left-wing register, Jean Baudrillard saw in the mullahs' inspection of the revolution a proof of vitality. In his view, Iran presented itself as

> the sole active de-stabilizer of the two great powers' terrorism and strategic monopoly. [...] Whether it is at the price of religious 'fanaticism', moral 'terrorism', or medieval 'barbarity', so be it, it doesn't matter. [...] No doubt only violence that is ritual but not at all archaic, the present violence of a religion, of a tribalness that rejects the models of free Western sociality, could launch such a challenge to the order of the world.[11]

In this respect, Simone de Beauvoir – even though along with Sartre and Foucault she was a member of the support committee for Ayatollah Khomeini, who was then living in exile in Neauphle-le-Château, near Paris – showed more reactiveness in March 1979, when a delegation of French feminists went to Teheran to look into respect for the rights of women. Divided on the question of the veil – some of them agreed to wear one to meet with the Ayatollah, while others refused – they called de Beauvoir, who had remained in Paris. She advised them to refuse to wear the veil. On 22 March, she wrote the following letter in support of Kate Millett, whom the new regime wanted to expel:

> today, the condition of women as such is in question, and that is what motivates our concern. Up to now, all revolutions have asked women to sacrifice their demands to the success of an action conducted essentially or uniquely by men. I support Kate Millett's wish and all my comrades who are in Teheran at this time: let this revolution be an exception; let the voice of this half of the human race be heard. The new regime will also be a tyranny if it fails to take their desires into account and does not respect their rights.[12]

5

An Unnatural Marriage

The era which dares to claim that it is the most rebellious that has ever existed only offers a choice of various types of conformity. The real passion of the twentieth century is servitude.

Albert Camus, *The Rebel*[1]

The image of Islam as a revolutionary force dates from the French orientalist Louis Massignon, who thought that solidarity with other religions ought to provide a counterweight to atheism and the de-Christianization of the Western masses.[2] Half a century later, some progressives see the junction with Islamic fundamentalism as an opportunity for their movement to catch a second breath, even if it is an unnatural marriage. Thus we see die-hard feminists seeking to minimize rape so long as it is committed by immigrants against European women. Let us return for a moment to the events in Cologne on New Year's Eve 2015: they crystallized a fascinating interpretive dispute. A former Socialist Party apparatchik, Caroline De Haas, the founder of *Osez le féminisme!*, said this about the facts in a tweet on 7 January 2016: 'those who tell us that the sexual attacks in Germany are due to the arrival of migrants: go dump your racist shit somewhere else'. The reasoning is powerful. Never has the schizophrenic relation between feminism and anti-racism been so striking. The male in rut is guilty only if he is white, heterosexual, and Western. The others are exculpated in advance, out of post-colonial remorse. A Belgian feminist, Sofie Peeters, who made a documentary film on harassment in the streets of Brussels, was caught in the same dilemma: 'that was my great fear, how to deal with this theme without making a racist film? [...] I don't like saying it, but in 95 per cent of the cases we're talking about foreigners [...] Muslims have a rather insistent behaviour with regard to sexuality: for a woman, wearing a skirt is already pretty risqué.'[3]

In the old days, it was forbidden to criticize the USSR for fear of playing into the hands of imperialism; that was how the totalitarian lie was able to prosper for such a long time. Now denial prevails. Let us recall that the day after the attacks in Cologne, the city's mayor, Henriette Reker, suggested that women keep an 'arm's length distance' from people they don't know, in order to avoid problems and not to arouse sensitive men who are unused to Westerners' sexual freedom. For left-wing feminists, the important thing is to drown the events in Cologne in the deep waters of equivalence. 'Depending on the origin of the aggressors, might there be victims of rape who are more worthy of support than others? Every day, from Cologne to Paris, from Beijing to New York, from Cairo to Rio de Janeiro, in the northern hemisphere and in the southern, men, of varying height and corpulence and from all sorts of social origins, attack and rape women', we read in a communiqué issued on 12 January 2016 by the *Osez le féminisme!* collective under the title: 'For every woman attacked, our indignation is total'. The dodge is pretty crude and it isn't clear that it will calm the victims. But we live in Europe, the communiqué goes on, 'in patriarchal societies where it is hard to be a woman'. So we must not 'instrumentalize these crimes', or think that macho violence is an event alien to our societies: 'The origin of the aggressors should not make us hesitate to denounce these aggressions, but we also condemn any form of racist recuperation of this event that harms women who are victims of rape or harms women's rights in general. Fighting patriarchal violence must be a priority 365 days a year. Indignation must not be selective, because feminism cannot have a variable geometry.' This argument reminds us of countless others made during the Cold War: when people urged support for dissidents in the USSR and in Czechoslovakia, it was strongly suggested that they not forget the people oppressed by American imperialism in Africa, Asia, and Latin America. To take committed action nowhere, all you have to do is commit yourself everywhere.

A little differentiation in this domain wouldn't hurt: the *Osez le féminisme!* collective might have reminded us that the everyday life of a woman in Paris, Brussels, or Stockholm is easier than it is in Riyadh, Islamabad, or Teheran, and that, after all, in Western countries a whole battery of very severe laws punishes crimes against women and children. That is what is called the rule of law. When German women are raped, it seems to some people more urgent to denounce the possible racism of those who name the aggressors than to provide help to the women who have been attacked. As for the militant communist Clémentine Autain, who was herself raped at knife-point at the age of twenty-three,[4] her sole response to the events in Cologne was the following tweet: 'between April and September 1945, 2 million German women were raped by soldiers. Was Islam to blame for that?' Apart from the arbitrary figures – corroborated by what historian? – what is the relation between the Soviet soldiers occupying the eastern part of the Reich, after four years of war, and the migrants welcomed with open arms by Angela Merkel's Germany? The disproportion is total and the situations are not comparable. Not only is this tweet fatal for our 'feminists', but it shows how much their reaction oscillates between denial and embarrassment. They slip away when we expect them: their hearts waver between the women raped and the rapists.

What is stupefying in these recantations is the extent to which a part of the left is prepared to trample on the left's own values. The conversion of certain periodicals to the market has to be compensated for by a frenzied cultural radicalism. If the French communist and socialist parties still make some use of critical reason when faced by radical Islam, Third-Worlders and Trotskyists often compound the moral debacle by abdicating their intelligence. Their compulsive anti-racism prospers in a progressivism that is completely falling apart and has long since abandoned any progress. Denouncing possible racism before seeking to protect women is a calamitous inversion of priorities. What is anti-racism today? The love of the Other pushed to the point of sacrificing oneself or one's family and friends. Obligatory fraternity with all of humanity, except with one's own culture. Because there is a single enemy: the white heterosexual man, heir to the DWEM, the Dead White European Male, as they say on American campuses. Thus the equality of men and women, the saving doubt, the critical mind, everything that was traditionally associated with an enlightened position, are all trampled underfoot. Only the racism turned against us is legitimate: we have to approve in the Other what we reject in ourselves. *Tolerance toward others also has to tolerate their intolerance toward us.*

Thus out of love for Islam, a certain halal left falls into a complete idolatry with regard to the Islamic veil, praised to the skies in a return of an old Romantic value: exoticism. People become ecstatically infatuated with the Salafists' whole mode of dressing, their orientalising get-up, just as in the nineteenth century people grew ecstatic over odalisques and harems. The typical neo-colonial sentimentality with regard to veiled women or bearded men, and the deification of archaisms rediscovered in the name of the Other, recall the remonstrances addressed to nationalist intellectuals by imperial administrators.[5] To the point that, for certain intellectuals, a Muslim woman who is not veiled and who is proud of it can only have sold out to the colonial authorities.[6] These ultra-conscientious persons would be prepared to cover the whole female sex in order to display their convictions. An emancipated North African girl is a traitor who has escaped her cultural origin 'by simply blow-drying her hair' and become the object of a 'compassionate racism' on the part of the media.[7] Another example: Esther Benbassa, a member of the European Senate who belongs to the Ecology/Greens party and also teaches at the Sorbonne. On 6 April 2016, in an op-ed piece in the newspaper *Libération* concerning a polemic against the Islamic fashion called 'modest fashion', she wrote that the veil is no more alienating than the miniskirt: 'All the women who wear short skirts and the sexy clothes prescribed by fashion (often designed by men) are not particularly emancipated, either.' Because all women are alienated, subjected to the dictates of fashion, the veil should be tolerated, and those who find some benefit in it, 'whether as a marker of identity or of religious conviction, should be respected'. The argument is strange: we know that in countless Muslim countries women are beaten, imprisoned, and vilified by the vice squad if they refuse to wear the veil, whereas the miniskirt has never been obligatory in Western countries. But we absolutely have to reject in tandem both the *niqab* and the miniskirt (or the G-string, another *bête noire*, I dare say, of the fundamentalists' friends), both of them forming 'symbolic enclosures' (Pierre Bourdieu).

Although the scarf conceals a woman's hair, it is above all a strategy of visibility: it distinguishes 'our' women from yours, the saved from the damned, the modest from the sluts, and makes it possible to count them up, so that it is a militant act, a demonstration of strength, the standard of an avant-garde that wants to win hearts and minds. To cover one's head is to break, overtly, with the rest of society, as Hani Ramadan, the brother of Tariq Ramadan and director of the Islamic Centre in Geneva, frankly pointed out: 'A woman without a veil is like a two-euro coin, it passes from one hand to another.'[8] Conversely, the academic Abderrahim Hafidi asks the Muslims of France to 'understand that some clothing behaviours, notably wearing the full-body religious gown, signifies for our fellow citizens who are not Moslems a refusal to live together, by barricading the wearer in a posture of exclusion'.[9] And again, the rector of the mosque of Bordeaux, Tareq Obrou, a former member of the Muslim Brotherhood, emphasizes the point to which wearing the Islamic veil is an ambiguous and minor prescription based on Hadiths of the Prophet whose authenticity is not certified. In this case he recommends a 'moderate religious visibility'.[10]

The veil, the burqa, and the burkini are tools for taking control of the public space, they are tracts calling for sedition. There is a kind of immodesty in this display of religious signs, since one's faith and convictions are thrown in the faces of others. What is called 'the re-awakening of Islam', noted for the past half-century, is perhaps only the syndrome of a faith that has already been eroded by modernity, and that prefers rigidity and identitarian conflict to reform. Fundamentalism operates chiefly at the level of appearances: in Beirut, in the 1980s, some Shiite groups were already paying young students almost a hundred dollars a month to wear the veil to the university. It is true that for many women the scarf is a kind of compromise between tradition and modernity (Fethi Benslama), a way of reconciling security and freedom, of going about their lives without upsetting their families and their communities. It is also true that the 'hijabistas', who are often elegant and wear make-up, make use of this head-covering as an object of aesthetic attraction, to do their errands or go to a café. But reducing the veil to a matter of fashion is deceptive, because it is anything but anodyne and optional. In Muslim countries, including Turkey as soon as one leaves urban centres, it is practically obligatory for girls, who are forced to wear it, sometimes from the age of eight, to bury themselves in this shroud. It would be grotesque to forbid it in our cities and our streets, but we must not be duped concerning the message it is sending and rush to help veiled women as though they were the last cohort of the desperate.

The fundamentalists' friends affirm that we have to undertake an inversion of values recalling that of Orwell's *Nineteen Eighty-Four* and its Newspeak: chains are freedom, hunger is abundance, oppression is emancipation. Thus the veil's defenders, who are themselves adversaries of 'Islamophobic feminism', see it as a strategy for wrenching away from the unknown colonial unconscious, another model of emancipation that opens the way to 'a radically dissonant interpretation of the hijab'.[11] The more hidden women are, the more they are free! It's possible that what fascinates our contemporaries so much in the religion of the Prophet is also *the giddy feeling of regression*. It allows us, without repudiating ourselves and even with the appearance of anti-racism, to oppose or to forget the Enlightenment's most cherished values. Hence, through this religion, we can make a great leap backwards, such as is desired by the most punctilious obscurantists. An imagined return to an old-regime society. We have really changed paradigms: in the eighteenth century, the Orient of sensual pleasure became the Orient of militant prudery, whereas the West that, up to the middle of the twentieth century, incarnated the repression of the body, came to incarnate instead, in fundamentalist propaganda, unfettered vice and depravity. The fact that today part of the left is militating for a return to concealing and imprisoning women is an astonishing bit of news. Tired of the freedoms it has granted itself over the past half-century, the Western world seems to be abdicating from them in order to fall into the arms of a basic but soothing cult: Salafism and its variants. Allegiance is pledged to the 'new Savonarolas' in order to lighten the burden of our independence. A phantasm of great repose, vaguely reformulated in terms of anti-imperialism, haunts the old left-wing groups, exhausted after so many lost battles and shattered hopes. The same people who have for forty years saluted the contraction of the domain of prohibitions and the expansion of the sphere of freedoms are now applauding the inverse phenomenon when it is proposed by Muslims. May our achievements perish if the Quran challenges them!

Good people, don't worry, your anxiety is only a fantasy. Islamization is a myth based on a collective obsession, Raphael Liogier tells us, comparing the Salafists to the Amish, that picturesque North American Anabaptist tribe fond of horse carriages, long beards, and crinoline petticoats.[12] 'The pseudo-scholarly nonsense about the Quranic roots of terrorism is of no interest', explains the expert Olivier Roy – who in fact does not speak Arabic and is not overly scholarly. Continuing this line of thought, he compares, 'mutatis mutandis', the Taliban's destruction of the Buddhas of Bamiyan in 2001 to the Swiss who want to get rid of minarets but not restrict religious freedom.[13] The sophistry is delicious, but it says only one thing: nothing is serious. What should we call these hypnotizers, active or passive? Righters of vision, as there are righters of wrongs. They tell us in countless ways: what you see isn't what you think. Let us tell you exactly how it is; we know, whereas you are wallowing in 'holy ignorance'.[14]

However, this remark has to be qualified: on the one hand, a very large part of the secular, republican left resists this retreat. On the other hand, it is often conservatives, or even 'reactionaries', who prove reluctant when faced with bearded doctrinarians, whereas too many 'progressives' acquiesce, in the name of tolerance, in the reduction of our prerogatives. A fascinating paradox: the conservatives defend not only a set of individual rights, the contemporary global citizen's right to do as he pleases, but also the civilizing base on which modernity has been built. Against cultural relativism and facile hedonism – which so easily turns into Puritanism – they want to protect traditions, a spirituality, a historical continuity that is just as important as our freedoms. Let us not forget that in the late 1930s it was two men who were on the right, according to our current criteria – de Gaulle and Churchill, one of them a monarchist, the other a Tory – who were the first to perceive the abomination of National Socialism and to make a stand against it. If historical lucidity consists in conceiving the event and remaining equal to what happens, then let us concede that left-wingers have generally failed in confronting Islamic terrorism. Where today are the International Brigades analogous to those that went to Spain in 1936, that the American philosopher Michael Walzer calls for, and that would stand up to Islamo-fascism?[15] The future will remember that in the twenty-first century, a large part of the Western intelligentsia made common cause with fundamentalist totalitarianism, just as their elders had communed with Nazism and communism.

6

The Victim's Guilt,
the Murderer's Innocence

> What can you say to a man who tells you that he prefers
> to obey God rather than men, and who is consequently
> sure that he deserves heaven for murdering you?
> Voltaire, *Philosophical Dictionary*, art. 'Fanaticism'[1]

Let us go a step further: the same culture of excuse
is equally applicable to mass murders. How can they
be exonerated? The arsenal of justifications seems
inexhaustible, even down to abjection. The most extrav-
agant acrobatics are then required. Thus the sociologist
Geoffroy de Lagasnerie explains the Paris attacks of 13
November 2015 at the Bataclan night club and in the
cafés of the eleventh arrondissement (130 dead, several
hundred wounded) by the fact that 'sidewalk cafés are
one of the most intimidating places for young people
from ethnic minorities. [...] A space where you don't
dare sit down, where you're not made welcome, where
you're not served, or, if you are served, it's expensive.
One of the most traumatizing places [...] Ultimately
you can say that they've slapped Jihadist words onto
an act of social violence that they felt when they were

sixteen.'[2] This real-time revisionism suggests an interesting reversal: the killers in the cafés were traumatized
people, and the customers who died under their fire
were privileged people. Conclusion: the victims were
murderers who didn't know they were murderers, and
the killers were unfortunate victims. Incidentally, didn't
a collective of Danish artists organize, in May 2016, an
exhibit in Copenhagen called 'Martyrs' that honoured
the el-Bakraoui brothers, who carried out suicide attacks
in Brussels, and one of the terrorists at the Bataclan?
How does a society come to celebrate those who want
to destroy it? By a symbolic manipulation of slaughters,
by a Stockholm syndrome reformulated in terms of
subversion. Rarely has the intellectual class deployed
such efforts to justify its submission. In the *Revue
du crieur*, the organ of the Mediapart website, Blais
Wilfert-Portal explained that 'the praise of sidewalk
cafés and the French way of life, "supposedly joyous
and festive, bawdy and mischievous in a kindly way,
tolerant and cosmopolitan", is not as "innocent" as
it seems. It is part of the repertory that has been
commonly mobilized since the nineteenth century when
"the nation is in peril" and is connected with more
explicitly aggressive forms of chauvinism.'[3] Defending
the French way of life is 'another kind of terrorizing
injunction [...] with all that that can imply in the way
of obligatory unanimism, the muzzling of legitimate
manifestations of criticism, of protest, etc., in short, an
atmosphere of censorship, formal or informal'. In other
words, going to have a drink in a bistro, kissing your
girlfriend, ordering a meal is another form of terrorism;
as for waving a French flag or hanging it off your
balcony, that is tantamount to attaching yourself to
the three dark moments in French history, 'World War
I, Vichy, and the colonial wars, all of them connected
in more or less explicit ways with dictatorship and
massive efforts to exert social control'. In short, 'the

French art of life' is susceptible to all sorts of 'identitarian manipulations', and behind the friendly face of restaurants, behind the smiles and the kisses exchanged among lovers, one can glimpse the terrible shadow 'of an iron cage'. If the first intellectual we cited here exonerated the killers by covering them with the benevolent shadow of social traumatism, the second limits himself to blaming the victims, past or future. Aren't you ashamed to go to a café and to associate yourself with the three dark moments in French history? Watch out: having a glass of wine in a bar will soon be tantamount to committing a nationalist crime. The tricolour way of life is questionable by nature. We already knew that ordering sausage with your aperitif was a sign of being on the far right politically. Now it is everything eaten in France that must be regarded with suspicion, 'to the great displeasure of the purists of traditional restaurant fare', as the militant ethnicist Rokaya Diallo explains: not only the ham-and-butter baguette but also the very French *blanquette de veau* have to be balanced by couscous, the kebab sandwich and halal food.[4] To change people's mentalities, you have to attack the stomach first.

What is going on that is causing good minds, people who are no stupider than others, to go off the rails in this way? Let's call it by a simple name: the self-hatred that I mentioned back in 1983,[5] present in the Western intelligentsia of the twentieth century provided it was justified by the Revolution, the Communist Party, or the Third World. But also the spirit of collaboration that appeared during the Second World War. Shortly after the attacks at the offices of *Charlie Hebdo*,[6] the far left, the New Anticapitalist Party (NPA), the French Communist Party (but without its political bureau), and the Front de gauche (but without Jean-Luc Mélenchon) could think of nothing better to do than to organize, for the end of February 2015, a meeting at the Bourse de

Travail in Saint-Denis to denounce 'Islamophobia and the securitarian climate of war' (with, among others, the Union of Islamic Organizations of France, which is close to the Muslim Brotherhood and the Parti des Indigènes de la République, a small identitarian group that is anti-feminist, anti-Zionist, and homophobic). *Charlie Hebdo*'s cartoonists and several members of the police force had just been assassinated in cold blood, and Jewish customers guilty of being Jews had just been killed in a kosher supermarket, but the organizers of the meeting in Saint-Denis rushed to denounce an alleged 'Islamophobia'.

To return to the massacres of November 2015 at the Bataclan and in the streets of the eleventh arrondissement, the great minds were, let's admit it, overwhelmed: for the Maoist Alain Badiou the murders were explained, of course, in a Pavlovian manner, 'by the aggressive emptiness of Western domination, of globalized capitalism, and the states that are its servants'.[7] Another philosopher, Michel Onfray, arguing on the basis of his intellectual superiority to journalists, who are prisoners of the short term, explained that these killings were the responsibility of the French state, which is guilty of pursuing an 'Islamophobic policy' alongside the United States, and is reaping what it sowed.[8] An old Third-Worldist refrain: the liberal capitalistic and imperialist West is guilty of causing everything bad on Earth, the assassins are soldiers, the terrorists are resisting our drones, our bombers. ISIS is a state that has a right to exist and with which we should negotiate a truce (the Islamic State's militants have in fact thanked the 'infidel' Michel Onfray and made him their darling, as was revealed by David Thomson, a journalist specializing in jihadism). The forfeiture is all the more saddening because it proceeds from a mind that we had earlier known as sharper.[9]

After the massacre in Nice on 14 July 2016, which caused eighty-six deaths when a man drove a truck into the crowd on the Promenade des Anglais, another philosopher, Jean-Luc Nancy, wrote in *Libération* on 18 July: 'We have to blame ourselves, our universal quest for power that is never satisfied. We have to stop and dismantle the mad trucks of our supposed progress, of our fantasies of domination, and our commercial obesity.' Dismantling the trucks: that is sure to console the victims' families. In the same spirit, we will have to deprive our cars of wheels, our trains of rails, our planes of wings, our knives of blades, and our forks of tines, since these are all objects capable of killing people. Another sage, Edgar Morin, who has weathered all the battles and is weary of the hysteria of war, summed up this thought in a tweet from September 2016: 'Barbarians kill indiscriminately by suicide attacks, civilized peoples kill indiscriminately by missiles and drones.' The die is cast, everything is equally valid. How strange: these thinkers, avowed atheists, are reinventing the old Christian notion of original sin.

I am attacked, therefore I am guilty. A mechanism of exculpation is operating that imputes to Europe and the United States most of Islam's crimes and turns its belligerence toward us into aggressiveness on our part. An arduous, crazy enterprise that has a symptomatic value but is made possible by multiple anathemas and inaccuracies.

In their turn, believers, even the greatest of them, can also go off the tracks. For example, questioned in the airplane that was bringing him back from Poland after World Youth Day on 31 July 2016, Pope Francis said regarding the recent attacks that had plunged France into mourning:

> I don't like to talk about Islamic violence because as I leaf through the newspapers I see violent acts committed every day, even in Italy: this person kills his fiancée, that

one kills his mother-in-law, and another... and they
are baptized Catholics! They are violent Catholics.
If I speak of Islamic violence, I have to speak about
Catholic violence [...] Like a mixed salad, it includes
all kinds [...] Terrorism grows when there is no other
choice, and at the centre of the world economy there is
the god Money, and not the person, man and woman,
that's the first terrorism.[10]

It's odd that the pope confuses fanaticism and materialism, which are two different orders. It's true that
Francis had already distinguished himself by making a
striking commentary after the assassinations at *Charlie
Hebdo*: 'if a great friend of mine speaks badly about
my mother, he can expect to get socked, and that's
normal'.[11] A strange reflection that is not very much
in accord with the Gospels and that proceeds more
from Latin *machismo* than from elevated theological
thought. With such bar-room talk, we are far from John
Paul II or Benedict XVI.

The culture of excuse is first of all a culture of
contempt: thinking to exonerate whole groups, it
infantilizes them. The jihadists are reduced to their
social conditions; far from being murderers, they are
archangels for whose crimes we are responsible.[12] They
are draped in the mantle of the persecuted, the psycho-
paths, the unstable. Every crime, every slaughter, every
bombing attack in France, in Germany, or in the Near
East is supposed to be partly our fault, and ought to lead
us to beat our breasts. In the ideology of absolution, the
act is now only a symptom. It is dissolved, literally, like
sugar in water, in the circumstances that surround it.
Killers, suicide bombers, are never responsible, because,
having been born from the soil of contempt, poverty,
and exploitation, they are only its products, desperate
people who felt an urgent need to kill as many others
as they could. However, there comes a time when

such individuals' aberrations can be attributed only to themselves: making them the unconscious puppets of the great powers amounts to exonerating them on the cheap. The friend of the oppressed shows a condescending paternalism toward his protégés: he denies them access to autonomy because he never makes them responsible for their acts, any more than he credits them with their individual successes. To those who attribute terrorism to economic inequalities in the Near East, to global warming, or to American or European interventions, let us oppose the wise counsel offered by the dean of the law school in Qatar: the only way to combat al-Qaeda or ISIS is to substitute for theirs another theology, other spiritual values that refute their own.[13] Religion is the main issue.

Beneath the surface, the far left and radical Islam agree on one point: they want to destroy this society, to be redeemed by the immigrant, by the foreigner who will come to regenerate our old, exhausted nations. We see this in the figure of the 'reconverted' all those who have traded their revolutionary illusions for the Quranic message: for example, the former Maoist Olivier Roy, already cited, who has substituted one religion for another, and specializes in defending 'moderate' fundamentalism'.[14] An indefatigable and talented advocate of orthodoxy, he reserves his ammunition for Muslim deserters, policies of de-radicalization, and, above all, potentially totalitarian secularity.[15]

What is the impact of these intellectual proclamations? So far as the public at large is concerned, it is no doubt minimal, but its influence on the media and the politicians who listen to these influential figures is real. The latter represent the oligarchy that imposes its views on the people; they are part of the elite that thinks, speaks, and decides for others. Whatever happens, even the worst, on the left (and on the far right) there will always be people authorized to tell us that we deserve what happens to us. Thanks to Marxism-Salafism, violence speaks the language of peace, fanaticism that of love. Everywhere, the *preachers of shame*, the professionals of voluntary servitude, work hand in hand with the *preachers of hate*. It is a strange sight to see frenzied anti-clerical writers losing all common sense when confronted by fundamentalist religious nuts. The Western far left and political Islam are both haunted by the same fantasy of recapitulation. The last battalions of the 'final struggle' join the feverish crowds of the 'final religion'. Just as the Quran claims to be the revelation that invalidates Christianity and Judaism by absorbing them, communism claims to move beyond the market economy and bourgeois society. The former does not understand why Jews and Christians persist in error, while the latter wants to take revenge for the historical setbacks suffered by Bolshevism.

Part III

Are Muslims the Equivalent of Jews?

7

From the Principle of Equivalence to the Principle of Substitution[1]

Do not consider it a breach of faith to kill them.
The breach of faith would be to let them carry on.
Abu Ishaq, a Hispano-Arab poet, writing before the
Granada pogrom of 1066.[1]

How can you acquire titles of nobility as a victim?
How can you gain access to the ultra-exclusive club of
the oppressed? *By becoming a contender for the world
pariah title.* The first step: affiliate yourself with one
of these groups, first to equal it, then to eliminate it.
Edward Said, an American polemicist and professor,
was the first to draw a parallel between Jews and
Muslims: in his book *Orientalism*, published in 1978,
he pointed out that the cartoons that appeared in the
Western press after the 1973 Yom Kippur war and
the oil embargo that followed it represented Arabs
with hooked noses standing around a gasoline pump:
'clearly Semites'. His conclusion: 'Popular anti-Semitic
animosity smoothly shifted from the Jew to the Arab
because the image is almost the same.'[2] The hostility
toward Islam in the Western world is supposed to be

fed by the same sources as anti-Semitism, even though
the image of the Jew has been transformed since the
creation of the state of Israel and its victories over
Arab armies. Now Jews are seen not as persecuted
but as persecutors. Thus the time has come for the
Muslim to take the place left vacant by the Jew. (In
2000, Said joked in the Israeli newspaper *Haaretz*
that he was the last Jewish intellectual in the region,
the last of Adorno's disciples: 'a Palestinian Jew'.) For
his part, the historian Enzo Traverso explains that, 'in
the new racism, Islamophobia plays the role that used
to be played by anti-Semitism': the rejection of the
immigrant, seen since the colonial period as the Other,
the invader, the foreign body that cannot be assimilated by the national community. Now the spectre of
terrorism is substituted for that of Judeo-Bolshevism.

> From this point of view, Islamophobia fits perfectly
> into what could be called the anti-Jewish archive [...] a
> repertory of stereotypes, commonplace images, repre-
> sentations, and accusations that convey a perception
> and an interpretation of reality that are condensed and
> codified in a stable, continuous discourse. A discursive
> practice that is capable of being transferred to a
> different object, anti-Semitism has therefore transmi-
> grated toward Islamophobia.[3]

The use of the word 'therefore' (*donc*) is interesting,
because it implies a logical connection that is more
postulated than it is demonstrated. Here we are in the
theory of the great replacement imagined by others
with regard to immigration. It is necessary at all
costs that Islamophobia replace or even supplant anti-
Semitism, which ultimately becomes boring because
of its perpetual rebirth. As one internet user wrote,
commenting on Traverso's book in the Mediapart
site's space for free expression: 'Jews are no longer

pariahs [...] but pariah peoples still exist. In the Near East, the Palestinian people, and in France, Muslim men and women, whose scarves and excessively long gowns are appallingly persecuted. [...] Fidelity to the tragic memory of the *shtetl* and *Yiddishland* now leads through the defence of Muslim women hounded by the belligerent secularism of the Republic.'[4]

New blood is needed in the little, closed world of racism: since 1945 there has been bitter competition among its various camps, which have been unable to find a federating narrative that links them. Anti-racism has become communitarian, and each group – blacks, Arabs, Jews, Asians, gays, and women – defends its own preserve. Few people know that yellow marks to designate Jews were imposed by a caliph in Baghdad in the ninth century. They are the ancestor of the yellow star of sinister renown (Christians were supposed to wear blue, in recognition of their status as a minority, as *dhimmis* in the Muslim state, which gave them protection in compensation for a restriction of their rights and a poll tax).[5] But yellow, which in the Muslim world lacked the symbolic intensity it had in twentieth-century Europe, has acquired, since the Holocaust, a cherished status: that of the damned. In 1994, at Grenoble, young Muslims already marched to protest the planned prohibition on wearing the Islamic scarf in schools and public buildings, and they did so by wearing an armband representing the Islamic crescent in yellow against a black background, accompanied by the words: 'When will it be our turn?' – a clear allusion to the yellow star that Jews had to wear during the Occupation. During the summer of the same year, when Islamist activists suspected of sympathizing with the Islamic Salvation Front – which was responsible for the civil war in Algeria – were placed in detention in a barracks in northern France, they immediately hung on the building's wall a banner that proclaimed:

'Concentration Camp'. In 2001 in Switzerland, the central Islamic council printed yellow decals that associated Islamophobia and the Holocaust, bearing a yellow star with eight branches and the inscription 'Muslim'. Thousands of stars were stuck up in all public places, including on the back of buses.

No matter how obscene the comparison might seem, becoming 'substitute Jews' seventy years after the Holocaust was the dream that a few dozen Iranian students realized on the University of San Diego campus when they wore yellow stars bearing the word 'Muslim'. The demonstration's goal was to accelerate public awareness of the rise of anti-Muslim racism. Before that, in 2009, a group of intellectuals concerned about the stigmatization of Muslims that might result from the debates about national identity ignited in France by Éric Besson and Nicolas Sarkozy compared the current French policy with that of the Third Reich, asking: 'After the yellow star, will it someday be necessary to wear a green star?'[6] However, such an analogy seems fragile. The Jews formed a people before they formed a religion: anti-Semitism is racialist by essence, it does not oppose Judaism as a belief but Jews for what they are. In addition, in the 1930s Jews were not carrying out bombings across the world in the name of the one true God, and they were not demanding separate rights but, on the contrary, assimilation (which is what the Sephardic Jews who came to France from North Africa in the 1960s, after decolonization, were also seeking).

Moreover, this postulated equivalence also neglects the historical alliance between National Socialism and the Grand Mufti of Jerusalem, Haj Amin al-Husseini, a fervent admirer of Hitler who in 1941 was granted the status of 'honorary Aryan'. Al-Husseini was Yasser Arafat's uncle and inspired the Muslim Brotherhood. As the creator of the Waffen-SS Handschar division in Bosnia-Herzegovina, whose soldiers were described as 'Germano-Muslims' by German propaganda, al-Husseini made genocidal anti-Judaism the cornerstone of his political programme (even though most Arab and Berber fighters were on the side of the Allies).

Paradoxically, this 'theft of the Holocaust' (Alvin H. Rosenfeld) and the desire on the part of some Muslims to be more Jewish than the Jews are contemporary with the rejection of the Hebrew state in the Middle East: 'The hatred for Israel is the most powerful aphrodisiac in the Arab world', the late king of Morocco, Hassan II, is supposed to have said. The Jews' monopoly on misfortune is an abuse that must be denounced. That is the opinion of Louis Farrakhan, the American leader of the Nation of Islam since 1981, who is also suspected of being involved in the murder of Malcolm X.[7] Nicknamed the 'black Hitler', and violently anti-Semitic, Farrakhan regularly accused Jews of having participated in the slave trade, and was followed on this terrain by the French humourist Dieudonné.

The Shoah has thus become for Jews the equivalent of Nessus' tunic: what was supposed to protect them burns them, it is an armour that consumes them from within. It has strengthened anti-Semitism as if it were a usurped privilege, whereas the legitimacy of the genocide is supposed to belong to others, the Palestinians, the Africans, the descendants of slaves, Muslims. A stupefying temporal telescoping: criticizing Islam, refusing to accept it in every respect, is supposed to be equivalent to nothing less than preparing for another Holocaust. Contemporary researchers such as James Pasto, Jonathan M. Herr, and Gil Anidjar thus seek to connect the construction of the 'Jewish problem' with that of the 'Muslim problem'. Christian Europe, the religious scholar Gil Anidjar claims, has conceived its enemy as 'structured by the Arab and the Jew, that is, by the relation that Europe maintains both with the

Arab and with the Jew'.[8] According to Edward Said, it
was Ernest Renan who, by constructing the 'science' of
orientalism, confirmed the Semite hypothesis invented
at the end of the eighteenth century by the historian
August Ludwig von Schlözer.[9] Said claims that Renan's
works on Semitic languages are part of 'a virtual
encyclopedia of race prejudice directed against Semites
(i.e., Moslems and Jews)'.[10] Thus there is supposed to
be a consubstantial link between the construction of
Europe and Islamophobia that is analogous to the one
between 'political Judeophobia [and] the construction
of nations in Europe in the nineteenth century'.[11] For
his part, Olivier Roy tells us that 'the arguments anti-
Semites used in the 1920s are repeated today against
Islam: cultural incompatibility and a greater loyalty
accorded to religion than to the nation'.[12] To those
who naively believed that contemporary Europe had
been constructed against its own demons, and first of
all against Germanic militarism, our analysts reply that
Europe seeks only to expel Muslims, seen as a foreign
body, from its territory, denying them any legitimacy,
any equality. A strange allegation, by the way: there are
more than 20 million Muslims in the European Union,
and for the past fifty years Europe has constantly
accepted new ones. What does it matter that the whole
history of this continent is also marked, as we have
seen, by 'the fascination with Islam'?[13] Whereas in the
Middle Ages this religion appeared to be a schism,
and not one of the most dreaded, in the Renaissance
it became a partner. The first chair of Arabic was
created in 1539 at the Collège de France, and in the
seventeenth century Islam became synonymous with
a refined civilization, a counter-model of tolerance
compared with medieval obscurantism. The Sublime
Porte impressed European courts. Louis XIV had to put
up with all the snubs inflicted on his ambassadors in
Constantinople, and both Pierre Bayle and Voltaire sang

the praises of Muslim civilization, deemed as elegant as it was voluptuous. Antoine Follant's translation of the *Thousand and One Nights*, published from 1704 to 1717, electrified the century of the Enlightenment, which dreamed of this happy sensuality so contrary to Catholic hypocrisy. Goethe wrote poems to the glory of Muhammad, and orientalism, which was a fantasy as much as a discipline, appeared as early as 1799.[14] How far we are here from the aggressive conventional images developed by demi-savants!

So why put anti-Semitism and Islamophobia on an equal footing, especially at a time when the former is flourishing all over the Arab Muslim world, under the name of anti-Zionism? To put it another way, why does everyone want to be a Jew these days, especially the enemies of the Jews? In order to accede in the imagination to the status of the outcast and to compare the defence of Islam with the struggle against Nazism. The Quranic faith alone is supposed to escape the kind of criticism that is normal for all other religions: it is untouchable, they are modifiable.

8

Exterminations Galore[1]

Generally speaking, we can distinguish between two main types of anti-Semitism: on the one hand, a religious anti-Judaism that is Christian and Muslim in inspiration, that accuses the people of Moses of having killed Christ and of persisting in error after the evangelical or Quranic revelation (the Jews are guilty of enjoying the privilege of anteriority, which has to be contested at any cost); on the other, a nationalist resentment that accuses stateless minorities of an agitation that is prejudicial to a country's good health. Since 1945, to these two classic grievances we have had to add a third, more unexpected, one: the envy of the Jew as a deportee, a paragon of misfortune after Auschwitz. Jewish suffering has become the benchmark and the Shoah the founding event on the basis of which crimes against humanity can be conceived. Whence the staggering growth in the use of the term 'genocide': saying that one is a victim of a genocide is a way of hijacking distress, of declaring oneself its sole legitimate owner. To put it another way, anti-Semitism constantly feeds on its own refutation. This insatiable, immemorial hatred is nourished by the very phenomenon that is supposed to limit it, the persecution of Jews.

Now Auschwitz is a crime to be blamed on its victims, as the former Labour Party mayor of London, Ken Livingstone, explained in spring 2016: 'Hitler was a Zionist'. Khadim Hussain, the Lord Mayor of Bradford and also a member of the Labour Party before his membership was suspended, raged against a British educational system that 'only tells you about Anne Frank and the 6 million Zionists that were killed by Hitler'. Many people compete with the Jews for the privilege of being annihilated, exclaiming: 'We are Auschwitz'. Let us note that numerous nations now base their self-conception on a founding catastrophe: the Armenians on the 1915 genocide, Ireland on the Great Famine from 1845 to 1852, Ukraine on the *Holodomor*, a famine provoked by Stalin in 1932–3, the Palestinians on the *Nakba*, Rwanda on the extermination of the Tutsis. Whence the ambivalence of negationism, which sometimes says that the Shoah did not happen, and sometimes that it happened but not to the people that we think, and that it has to be restored to other, more deserving, ethnic groups: Africans, Palestinians, Muslims. It is an inversion of the dead, not of the event itself, which has been detached from its temporal underpinnings and moved through history like a mirror, in a *reductio ad Hitlerum* in which colonialism, slavery, and imperialism are seen as logical steps toward the Third Reich. The event is too massive to be eluded, but it is redistributed according to the groups seeking to monopolize it.

By a monstrous misinterpretation, the Shoah has become an object of desire: it fascinates people like a treasure that they believe they can use to their advantage, and it feeds a mimetic rivalry. That is why any annoyance experienced by a minority is now re-transcribed in the language of the Holocaust, often with the intention of dislodging those already associated with it. Consider this statement made by Sir Iqbal Sacranie, the Secretary General of the Muslim Council of Britain until 2006, who proposed replacing Holocaust Memorial Day with Genocide Day: 'The message of the Holocaust was "never again" and for that message to have practical effect on the world community it has to be inclusive. We can never have double standards in terms of human life. Muslims feel hurt and excluded that their lives are not equally valuable to those lives lost in the Holocaust time.'[2] The idealization of deportees that took place after the war paved the way for their later denigration. *The Jewification of the Muslims automatically leads to the Nazification of the Israelis* (and, by extension, to that of all Jews described as 'Zionists', if they do not publicly repudiate Israel's policies). It is in this sense that the French Parti des Indigènes de la République accused François Hollande's socialist government of practising a 'state philo-Semitism', that is, of protecting French Jews, 'those cherished children of the Republic' appointed to defend 'the white body' and 'the racial infrastructure of the nation-state', instead of being concerned solely with the true humiliated group, the Muslims. (It also demanded, in a caricature of the secular spirit, that the Representative Council of French Jewish Institutions (CRIF) be separated from the state.)

The Second World War turns out to have invented a new pathology: victimism. Since certain words, including 'genocide', have remained radioactive, they have to be stolen from others. The slogan of the new negationism is: crimes against Muslims have taken place before your eyes, in Palestine and in Europe, but you don't see them, blinded as you are by the old afflicted groups, who have become the heirs of National Socialism. To repeat a famous formula, which is itself parodic, 'One genocide can hide another' (Serge Thion).[3] The Nuremberg Trials did not simply punish the guilty, they staged the enjoyment of an accursed privilege. The history of the crime against humanity is now that of its falsifications and misappropriations. Since 1945, the world has entered the great market of affliction, because the latter confers rights and especially an impregnable moral position. By raising the word 'Islamophobia' to the level of anti-Semitism, people can finally brandish their certificates of malediction as titles of nobility. Victimization is the pain-oriented version of privilege. If it suffices to call oneself oppressed in order to be in the right, everyone will fight to occupy that slot. Every conqueror likes to be seen as a martyr. No one admires the Shoah more than the revisionists, to the point of wanting to steal it from those who suffered from it.

In one of his articles, Bernard Lewis recalls a sinister little phrase that was circulating in the Near East before the Six-Day War in 1967: 'First the Saturday people, then the Sunday people'.[4] First the Jews, then the Christians. We know that the Quran accuses Christians of succumbing to polytheism by giving God a trinitarian dimension, the Father, the Son, and the Holy Spirit. As for the Jews, God grew weary of their sins and abandoned them to open the convenant to everyone and to confer election on the Arabs.[5] But the underlying fear persists that God might change his mind and once again grant his favour to the Jews. It seems that the Hebrew state, which its neighbours vowed to see disappear and which has endowed itself with a considerable military power, is withstanding the hostility better than was foreseen, and has even become a haven of peace and wealth in the middle of an Orient ravaged by anarchy. The country whose imminent demise has been predicted for sixty years is insolently prospering amid the ambient chaos. So that it can be seriously asked whether the Arab world will still exist thirty years from now (the great Syrian poet Adonis's prognosis is that Arab civilization, crushed by a regressive Islam, is dying). In the

Land of Islam, the Jew was simultaneously protected and scorned, called a pig, an ape,[6] treated as an inferior.[7] Now he is hated, vilified – and this is a promotion. The fury that the Hebrew state arouses comes from the fact that the Jew, who used to be sub-human, has become, in the course of half a century, an equal. This kind of reversal is intolerable. Let us add that if Israel did not exist, the Arab countries would be obliged to invent it in order to justify their failures. It constitutes the ideal scapegoat, invoked even to explain terrorism: according to certain conspiracy theory websites, the events of 11 September 2001 in New York and of 13 November 2015 in Paris were arranged by the Mossad. Even the creation of ISIS is sometimes attributed to the Israeli secret service. Despite the wealth of the Judeo-Islamic tradition, which has often been brilliant but also tragic, punctuated by as many marvels as pogroms, and despite the protection from which Hebrew communities once benefited, especially under the Ottoman Empire, it has to be admitted that a Jewish presence in the Land of Islam is practically no longer possible, except perhaps in a vestigial form.[8] Although the Arab conquerors at first respected the pluralist structure of countries in North Africa and the Middle East, the multi-denominational utopia of Andalusia, which was largely mythical, is dead. In our time it has become difficult for Jews in Europe to live in serenity in neighbourhoods where there is a Muslim majority. As for Christians, who have been the object of endless persecution and ethnic cleansing, they are perhaps living their last years in the Land of Islam, and are even threatened on French soil, as was shown by the killing of Father Hamel in his church at Saint-Étienne-du-Rouvray in July 2016.[9] In continental France, cathedrals and basilicas are guarded by the police or the army, and parish priests are equipped with a device that enables them to launch a 'terrorist attack alert'.

9

The Jew, An Accursed White

If a Muslim insults a Jew, the latter must bow his head and keep silent.

Edict issued by the Iranian mullahs of Hamadan, 1892[1]

What has happened to Jews since the creation of Israel? A pigmentary curse: they have become white. According to Enzo Traverso, in the United States Jews and blacks used to fight racism and colonialism in concert. Then the Jews, especially after 1948, crossed 'the colour line', got rich, and became 'whites', that is, oppressors![2] With the end of anti-Semitism, the Jew has joined the superior (white) race; with Israel, he caught the European disease of nationalism, and that is what doomed him. Having left the ghetto, he no longer embodies that 'negative alterity' that formerly made him unique. 'The internal outsider is no longer the Jew: it is now the Arab and the black, that is, the ex-colonized individual who lives in continental France and has become a French citizen.'[3] It is strange that this list never includes the Vietnamese, Cambodians, or Laotians, who were formerly subjects

of the French Empire and, along with the Chinese, have
been the objects of a genuine racism on the part of
people living in the working-class suburbs in France.[4]
It is true that French citizens of Asian origin have
never chosen the culture of complaint, but rather that
of work and effort. Obviously, they are not candidates
for the ideal victim. Let us leave aside Enzo Traverso's
racialist insanity. According to Pierre Tevanian, to be
white is to enjoy 'a pigmentary privilege' from which
neither blacks, nor Arabs, nor Muslims benefit.[5] It is
a social, symbolic comfort that has to be challenged at
any cost: 'Whites are in fact sick with a disease that is
called racism and that affects all of them, in different
ways, even – and I will return to this – if they are
not racists.'[6] The qualification is important: the white
person is afflicted by a metaphysical calamity. It is this
dis-ease that has to be purged no matter what. It is the
corrupting demon who has awakened, in every people,
the spirit of division and cruelty. Thus people will go so
far as to ban it from meetings opposing racism, and do
it for its own good: it is a deliberate ostracism carried
out in the name of anti-colonial and anti-imperialist
struggles.[7] They simply invert the National Socialist
rhetoric that exalted only Aryans. Here only 'whites',
with their 'chalk-white faces', are denigrated in order
to celebrate other skin colours by attributing all good
qualities to them. With this hysterical 'epidermization'
of the discussion, we remain right in line with the old
distinctions that emerged from slavery. Melanin vs.
leucoderma: here we see the rebirth of the obsession
with the pedigree, and people are once again compart-
mentalized into ethnic syndicates.

It's still the same thought, turned upside down like
an hourglass: there are superior 'races' and inferior
'races'; a struggle between races has replaced the class
struggle. 'To be white is to be raised in this twofold
imposture: the benefit of a privilege and the denial of

this privilege.'⁸ Extricating oneself from this imposture, according to Tevanian, requires 'a constant *askesis*'. But not everybody who wants to be Jean Genet can be, and endlessly excusing oneself for being 'a white hetero-sexual bourgeois' betrays a certain form of narcissistic ostentation. What a delight to be at the summit of human depravity, to be able to say that one is a 'renegade white', through 'partial identification', along with veiled women, illegal immigrants, and Islamists.⁹ Tevanian also calls the philosopher Abdennour Bidar, a French intellectual of Muslim culture and the author of a *Lettre ouverte au monde musulman* (3 October 2014),¹⁰ a 'merchant of fascism with a spiritual face': Bidar had in fact dared to describe Islam as threatened with a regression into obscurantism, and urged Muslims to turn toward tolerance and openness. The eternal bias of the ultra-left: it is always fixated on an obsolete barbarism, keeping its eyes on the National Socialism of yesterday the better not to see its contemporary versions. Whites are cursed, they incarnate humanity's negative colour, from which all evil flows. They inspire such disgust that a female novelist, eager to get rid of this accursed mob, describes the future human 'as beige, dark with brown hair. France, the whole world will crossbreed.'¹¹ The desire to eliminate the white 'race' in an undifferentiated mixture (just as gender theory would like to make the sexes disappear) has no parallel other than in supremacists' obsession with maintaining it in its purity. But to believe that generalized cross-breeding will escape any segregation, because everyone will bear the Other in himself, is to display a lack of realism. The distrust aroused among classification fanatics by crossbreeds, mulattos, and quadroons who feel neither black nor white suffices to dissipate this illusion. The fact is that anti-racism always pursues two contradictory objectives: mixture and diversity, universal non-distinction and the beauty of the multiple.

The writer Frantz Fanon, who hailed from the Antilles, liked to recall his philosophy professor's words: 'When you hear people denigrating Jews, prick up your ears, they're talking about us.' An anti-Semite was necessarily a Negrophobe, both Semites and blacks being objects of the same animosity. We know that in France as in the United States, blacks and Jews shared a solidarity as outcasts: they were the invisibles, especially in America, banished from the public space reserved for WASPs alone. This fine unity collapsed; Jews are no longer 'brothers in wretchedness' according to Frantz Fanon, but rather those whose tragedy, which took the form of pogroms and the Shoah, tarnishes my own tragedy and prevents me from being their brother. There were genocides before 1942, and the whole history of humanity is in one sense the history of a crime against humanity. It is as if the Holocaust had opened up a new space of interpretation. In one case, it is a founding event that allows us to see in a different way the extermination of the Amerindians in North and South America and of the Aborigines in Australia, the massacre of the Herero in Namibia by the Kaiser's troops, of the Armenians by the Turks, the crimes of colonialism (including Ottoman and Arab colonialism), and slavery in its three dimensions, inter-African, Asian, and transatlantic. In another sense, as we have seen, it is a dark theology that makes Jews the depositories of a treasure that has to be taken away from them. It is one thing to say that Auschwitz allows us to conceive mass crimes; that is the famous penal pedagogy that Karl Jaspers talked about regarding the Nuremberg Trials (which the Tutsis of Rwanda followed, for example). It is another thing to say that Auschwitz conceals our wretchedness and must be abandoned. The wounded memories compete in the name of the maximal affront of which each of them claims to be the depository, because it generates legitimacy.

Therefore the goal is to transfer Europe's moral debt from the Jew to the Muslim, and to put the former on the side of the white colonizer, via the Palestinians' suffering. Thus the West is supposed to become the Islamic world's eternal debtor. Jews are transformed into a metaphysical adversary, as Alfred Rosenberg already said in 1923; or, to borrow Hitler's words to Hermann Rauschning: 'there cannot be two Chosen People. We are God's people. These words settle everything.'[12] Following Enzo Traverso, Houria Bouteldja, who denies that he is an anti-Semite, commands Jews to repudiate Israel and any affinity with Zionism, for fear of being affiliated with the white rabble. In the space of fifty years, the Jews have 'passed from being pariahs to *dhimmis* of the republic for the nation-state's internal needs, and to Senegalese Tirailleurs for the needs of Western imperialism'.[13] Jews, the West's former scapegoat, have become, in their Zionist version, the paragon of colonialism. Thus they are exponential whites, quintessential whites. For them, the choice is as clear-cut as it is simple: either go over to the side of those other Semites, the Arabs, or support Israel and plunge into the abominable.

The relentlessness with which some 'progressive' groups trample on what they call 'whites', all the while explaining that there is no discrimination with regard to them, is strange. Whites are supposed to be the only ones guilty of having invented the hierarchy of races, and of having spread misfortune and hatred everywhere they went. It is painfully obvious that this racism exists. It is the anti-Semitism present in North Africa, in the Middle East, in our suburbs: it recycles the far right's old anti-Jewish hatred by way of the far left, focused on the denunciation of Israel. Here we find a specific characteristic of modernity: *in our time, true racism expresses itself in the words of anti-racism,* just as contemporary fascism is anti-fascist in its mode of expression. It begins by denouncing the old segregations the better to continue them, polish them, give them the guarantee and the lustre of subversion. The taboo has become the best propagator of the epidemic it is supposed to combat. The new racism always dons the clothing of the resistance to the brown plague the better to perpetuate the green plague. This new-look trend culminates in the anti-Zionism about which Vladimir Jankelevitch already said, in a book that appeared in 1986, that it was 'an unhoped-for windfall, because it gives you the permission and even the right to be an anti-Semite in the name of democracy! Anti-Zionism is anti-Semitism justified, finally made available to everyone. It is the permission to be democratically anti-Semitic. What if the Jews themselves were Nazis? That would be marvellous. It would no longer be necessary to feel sorry for them: they would have deserved their fate!'[14]

In the name of the fight against colonialism, the first duty of an anti-racist is to be an anti-Zionist. Thus we see appearing a newcomer in the political struggle, the 'anti-fascist anti-Semite', like those who desecrated a Jewish cemetery in Sarre-Union in February 2015, promising to fight Nazism down to the last ... Jew.[15] All Jews have to do is to stop supporting Israel, as the sociologist Laurent Mucchielli explains, deploring 'the inability of Jewish institutions in France to distance themselves from the Israeli state, which is the counterpart and the amplification of the inability of many Muslims to distinguish Israeli policy from the Jewish community in general'.[16] In other words, the Jews of France are solely responsible for their misfortunes. This makes it possible to minimize the crimes that have punctuated recent French history: over the past ten years, Islamists or people like them have killed no fewer than eleven French citizens because they were Jews.[17] Not to mention many other attacks, including that on a Jewish couple, in Creteil in December 2014, who were suspected of keeping a pile of money in their home, followed by the rape of the wife. Persons who were or who looked Jewish were insulted and sometimes even killed.[18] In the summer of 2014, cries of 'Death to Jews!' were heard in the centre of Paris during pro-Palestinian protest demonstrations. When Muslims are killed, it is, by a tragic irony, by other extremist Muslims, as in the case of the three soldiers executed by Mohammed Merah in March 2012 in Montauban and in Toulouse, or in that of the thirty people of Muslim ancestry (out of a total of eighty-six victims) cut down in Nice on 14 July 2016 by a truck driven by Mohamed Lahouaiej-Bouhlel, a thirty-one-year-old Tunisian affiliated with ISIS. Forced to decide between two minorities, many left-wing intellectuals, supporters of the Palestinian cause, preferred to abandon Jews (and Asians) to the benefit of Arabs and Africans. The former are supposed to be too favoured, even if an intense feeling of insecurity drives them to emigrate to Canada, the United States, or Israel. The fact that many Jews can no longer walk the streets in the suburbs wearing a Star of David or a kippa without risk of being attacked or insulted; the fact that Jewish children can no longer be educated in certain public schools where the majority of students are of North African descent, especially in the suburbs; and the fact that the Shoah can no longer be taught in many schools (as was revealed by the Obin Report in 2004),[19] were all explained by reference to the geopolitical situation and unrest among the young in the housing projects.

Europe and especially France have erected multiple moral and legal barriers to prevent the return of the foul Beast. But like the supporters of the Labour Party in England, they may at times practise an anti-Semitism by abstention, in the name of a laudable concern for equity. Anti-racism ends up turning into what it denounced, the detestation of a precise group, and this does more to weld together a community than do appeals to harmony and respect for all. In *Civilization and its Discontents*, Freud warned us that 'it is always possible to bind together a considerable number of people in love, so long as there are other people left over to receive the manifestations of their aggressiveness'. Because they enjoyed the privilege of coming earlier, the Jews remain the gold standard for racial hatred when that hatred no longer knows where to turn. Once the other scapegoats have been exhausted, the Jews are still there, a last resort. When will we see progressive pogroms?

10

A Semantic Racket

For the past half-century, many Arab regimes have reproduced all of Europe's anti-Jewish stereotypes as they were formulated from Karl Marx to Hitler, not forgetting Henry Ford and Roger Garaudy. *The Protocols of the Elders of Zion*, an anti-Semitic forgery confected by the czarist police, is a perpetual best-seller in the Middle East. It is sold on the streets in all Arab cities and even figures on the curricula of certain universities. It is the only Western graft that has really taken hold in this part of the world. Because the real Jew today, according to the *doxa*, wears a keffiyeh and speaks Arab; the other one is merely an impostor who has arrogated a title to property and has already lost 'the moral magistracy of the martyr' (Péguy). Although the Israel-Palestine question remains an open wound, over the past decade it has shifted from a universal conflict to a regional conflict, and is increasingly dwindling into 'a real-estate dispute over whose house this is'.[1] But for a whole ultra-left, it remains the focus of a battle between civilizations. Let us quote one sentence among many, taken from an interview with the former diplomat Stéphane Hessel, a staunch supporter of Hamas, published in the *Frankfurter Allgemeine Zeitung* in January 2011: 'The German occupation, compared with the current occupation of Palestine by the Israelis, was a relatively inoffensive occupation, setting aside the internments and the theft of artworks.' Thus the state of Israel is seen as having dethroned the Third Reich as the incarnation of barbarism. When the Jews oppress or colonize, not only are they transformed into Nazis but they behave worse than the Nazis, as Sheikh Ibrahim Mudeiris claimed in Gaza in 2005: 'The Jews are behind the suffering of nations.'[2] For Hani Ramadan there is a Zionist conspiracy to dominate the world, and Europe is supposed to have been 'infiltrated by Tsahal'.[3]

The prejudice according to which Arabs cannot be anti-Semites because they are Semites themselves is obviously deceptive: first of all because the word refers to a linguistic and not a racial category, and also because the word 'anti-Semite', which Wilhelm Marr forged in Germany in 1879, never referred to Arabs but solely to Jews and their projects of emancipation (though both Arabs and Jews are 'Semites' in so far as they speak Semitic languages).[4] After the creation of Israel, the Arab world reinvented Christian anti-Judaism, adapting it to the situation in the Near East, Islamicizing its lexicon, avoiding any distinction between Jews and Zionists, and peddling, regarding this people described as demonic and conspiratorial, the most repugnant images produced by National Socialist propaganda.

It was in 2001, during the ill-named World Conference Against Racism held in Durban, South Africa (where tracts glorifying Hitler were handed out), that this orientalized anti-Semitism was officially baptized. But it was, as Pierre-André Taguieff rightly put it, declared 'in the name of anti-racism and human rights'.[5]

Once the equivalence of anti-Semitism and Islamophobia was established, a subtle process of symbolic appropriation began. The goal was to evict the Jews in order to put the Muslims in their place. It's our turn, the latter said. That was, for example, what the writer Edward Said was expecting when Sartre and Simone de Beauvoir invited him to Paris in 1978 to attend a seminar on peace in the Middle East. The meeting took place at Michel Foucault's apartment. Said's disappointment was proportional to his expectations. De Beauvoir appalled him with her 'condescending stupidity' with regard to Islam, because all she did was protest against the wearing of the chador in Iran. Michel Foucault soon left the discussion; he was too favourable to Israel, as Said was later to learn from Gilles Deleuze. As for Sartre, who was old and frail, he spoke little, and always under the control of Benny Lévy, a.k.a. Pierre Victor, who had become his mentor; Lévy was the former director of *La Cause du Peuple* who had transformed into an Orthodox Jew. Said was expecting Sartre to make a formal declaration in favour of the Palestinians. But the following day, guided by his young secretary, Sartre limited himself to reading a short text in which he confirmed his support for the two-state solution and praised the attitude adopted by Sadat, who was prepared to make peace with Israel. Said was dismayed: Sartre did not depart from his classic philo-Zionism and did not show himself to be sensitive to 'the justness of the Arab cause' except in the case of Algeria. Said wondered if this lack of sensitivity to the Palestinian question proceeded from a lack of empathy with the Arab world, religious prejudice, or a sense of guilt with regard to the Holocaust.[6] Ten years earlier, Frantz Fanon's widow had asked François Maspero to remove Sartre's preface to *The Wretched of the Earth* in subsequent editions of the book: 'There is no longer anything in common between Sartre and us, between Sartre and Fanon', she wrote in 1967 in an Algerian newspaper. 'Sartre, who in 1961 dreamed of joining those who shape the history of humanity, has gone over to the other camp. The camp of the murderers. The camp of those who kill in Vietnam, in the Middle East, in Africa, in Latin America.'[7]

For a whole generation of activists, the Palestinian question had to be a natural outcome of decolonization. But for French intellectuals who had lived through the war, the Jewish question could not be simply swept away and replaced by a mythology that was no doubt legitimate, but did not have the same symbolic weight. Their successors did not have the same scruples, and starting in the 1980s the whole ultra-left swung over into an unequivocal condemnation of the state of Israel. Do not judge us, the fundamentalists say. You'd have to be Muslims to understand. Hence Islam, instead of performing its *mea culpa*, as the Catholic Church did at the time of Vatican II, between 1962 and 1965, instead of undertaking a re-examination of its history and its doctrine, and of the verses of the Quran and the Hadiths, seeks to present itself as the creditor of humanity as a whole. We owe it everything, as a consequence of the wrongs it has endured since the Crusades, colonialism, and the occupation of Palestine. Finally, it suffers from a bad and unjust image.[8] Just as the Quran claims to be the *summa* that includes and transcends the two earlier monotheisms, Islamophobia claims to be the global racism that includes all the others. Thus, a journalist explains, it has 'become the secret weapon of a diffuse social war', a 'racism without race' that fabricates illegals and also drives out gypsies (*sic*).[9] What is the relation between gypsies and the judgement one might make on the Prophet's religion? None, a priori, but the essential point is to describe Islamophobia as the modern figure of absolute evil. The attraction of the term is its plasticity, which allows it to be adapted to every period, every phenomenon, even climate change.

Its sycophants have elevated it to the first and final cause of the way the world works, almost a cosmic principle. This claim was made, self-importantly, by Ghassan Hage, a professor of anthropology at the University of Melbourne, at an MIT conference in May 2016: 'Global warming is accelerated by Islamophobia, the dominant form of racism today [...], which finds its source in the colonial form of capitalist accumulation.'[10]

How should we react to this semantic racketeering? First, by pointing out that we must not confuse different kinds of debts. These are debts that are made not to be reimbursed but recognized and transmitted. They are good debts that have to be honoured, and Europe has one with regard to Judaism, which has accompanied its history since the beginning, that is, since six centuries before Muhammad appeared in Arabia. Ultimately, Islam would be well advised to consider the debt that it itself has contracted with regard to humanity. The day when its highest authorities (in this case, Al-Azhar University in Cairo for the Sunni world) recognize the conquering and aggressive nature of their faith, ask to be pardoned for the holy wars committed in the name of the Quran, apologize for the colonial conquests in Spain, Europe, Africa, and Central Asia, as well as for the terrorist attacks committed in the name of God, will be a day of progress, first of all for Muslims, and it will help dissipate a great many people's suspicion of this sacrificial monotheism. Something tells us that this day is still far off. Let us add that Jewish and Christian fundamentalisms are no less grotesque. It is worrisome to see Donald Trump's Republican adminis-tration praised by the most narrow-minded evangelical churches, and Vice-President Mike Pence defending creationist ideas. In France itself, schismatic Catholics are challenging the achievements of Vatican II. In Israel, in the Mea Shearim neighbourhood (which the secular left calls 'Little Teheran'), ultra-orthodox Jews, the

Haredim ('the God-fearing'), who are often hostile to the Hebrew state, are sending their vigilantes against women not wearing enough clothes, in a striking imitation of the hypocrites on the other side. But apart from the fact that they are not carrying out bombings all over the planet, these fundamentalists remain a minority within their own religion and are limited by liberals and traditionalists.

This is all the more the case because the denominational division between the Quran's zealots and the others can also be interpreted as a division between the race of the saved and the race of the lost, between *Dar al-Islam*, the house of Islam, on the one hand, and *Dar al-harb*, the house of war, on the other. We are the lost, they are the elect. Moreover, the use of the term 'infidel' (*kufar*) to designate non-Muslims is strange, since Christianity speaks instead of 'non-believers'. There is something pejorative about the first term, as if it indicated a lesser degree of humanity. 'Unbelief is a single nation', says a formula attributed to the Prophet, and this inevitably leads to a division of the world into two groups. In turn, suicide bombers make another distinction: between themselves and the 'infidels', those who have strayed from the right path and have to be brought back to Truth by the sword, by fire, and by bombs. Each time, the group of the Pure grows more limited, leading to more segregations and massacres. That is the very definition of totalitarianism on the basis of religious assumptions.

Part IV

Are We Guilty of Existing?

I don't care if I'm killed in war. What will remain of what I have loved? As much as about people, I am talking about customs, irreplaceable intonations, a certain spiritual light. About eating breakfast under the olive trees on a farm in Provence, but also about Handel. [...] What matters is a certain arrangement of things. Civilization is an invisible good, because it bears not on things, but on the invisible links that connect one thing with another in this way and not in another.

Antoine de Saint-Exupéry, Letter to General X written on 31 July 1944, just before his death in combat.

11

The Criminalization of Reticence

France is now a Muslim culture. Islam is a French religion. You have the cultural ability to make French culture considered an Islamic culture among cultures.

Tariq Ramadan[1]

On 7 December 2015, a little more than three weeks after the terrorist attacks in Paris on 13 November that resulted in 130 dead, an editorial writer for the daily newspaper *Libération*, Luc Le Vaillant, described his fear on line 4 of the Paris Metro: a young female passenger wearing a crow-black abaya (a loose-fitting cloak or dress), her hands gloved, stood in the middle of the car attracting everyone's attention. She was between 25 and 30 years old, rather pretty, and had a shoulder bag slung over her shoulder that looked like it 'might be stuffed with TNT'. Everyone considered 'the possibility that there was an explosive chastity belt' hidden under this 'monotheistic cassock'. The author reassured himself by reflecting that this young person was probably going through a period of radicality as other people have a punk period, defy death, get high on coke or on prostitution. Nonetheless, in view of what had recently happened in Paris, he was afraid that she was displaying these sinister emblems in order to 'spray the sidewalk cafés with a Kalashnikov' or trigger a bomb in the Metro. Prudently, he finally decided to get out of the Metro at the Saint-Placide station.[2]

What had he written?! A few days later, faced by the protests, the newspaper's editor-in-chief, Laurent Joffrin, had to publish a front-page editorial defending his journalist. He pointed out that 'op-eds are by nature diverse and subjective, and do not commit the newspaper to the same extent that an editorial or a reporting article does'. The former head of the Collectif français contre l'Islamophobie (CCIF), Marwan Mohammed, regretted that this opinion piece had been published. He said that Luc Le Vaillant had 'described fantasies and anxieties that circulate in society'. No doubt: but isn't anxiety legitimate three weeks after a series of attacks in Paris that killed more than 130 people? Do we still have the right to feel afraid, legitimately, without being called a fascist, in an atmosphere of collective assassinations? The fear of disapproval in relation to the treatment of members of cultural minorities can seal our lips and make us, in spite of ourselves, accomplices in dreadful crimes. Consider the case of the social services and police forces in England in 2014 who were slow to dismantle a network of Pakistani sexual predators long known to them. The fear of being called racists justified their 'reluctance to identify the ethnic origin of the guilty parties'.[3]

That is the problem that arises when every criticism of Islam is assimilated to discrimination. Fundamentalism has understood Western guilt very well, and uses and abuses it. This is expressed by the official statutes of the Collectif contre l'Islamophobie en France: 'The CCIF fights in particular [...] Islamophobia understood as an irrational fear of Islam and Muslims, an active ill will toward Islam and those who practise it.'[4] Where does ill will begin, where does the irrationality of fear begin, in view of what we are experiencing? That is the whole problem. This fear has consequences: because of it, Muslims, in France or elsewhere, are said to feel stressed, to be forced to adopt constant strategies of avoidance, to conceal their observance of Ramadan, to submit to a hyper-control, to rely on a kind of *mektubism* (destiny), and to interiorize the rejection of which they are supposed to be the object.[5] What others would call the context of the attacks, the consequence of a crisis situation, is supposed to be described here as racism. We understand that part of the progressive camp subscribes to this analysis, because for decades being on the left has meant looking everywhere for reasons to be upset. The religion of compassion has everywhere replaced the sense of justice. We pile up grandiloquent words: the Other, the Foreigner, the Migrant, to emphasize the offences committed by France or other European nations. Praising foreigners while at the same time considering them French citizens is self-contradictory. We want foreigners to be our fellows, to become like us, and at the same time we emphasize their alterity!

From then on, the host society is supposed to abandon any attitude of suspicion or fear with respect to citizens of another religion.[6] It is up to it to make the effort. A report published in 2006 by the European Monitoring Centre on Racism and Xenophobia (EUMC) explains with a straight face that terrorist acts committed on American, Spanish, and British soil since 2001 are traumatizing not for the victims but for 'Muslims' and 'Arabs' and 'asylum seekers', whereas surveys conducted after September 11 in Europe showed no increase in the rejection of Muslims in Western public opinion.[7] A terrible hatred of Islam on the part of Americans and Europeans is fabricated, and is no more than a projection of the hatred that Islamic fanatics feel with regard to us (this was also the mechanism of National Socialist propaganda against Jews). Anti-racism is really the contraband flag waved by the fundamentalists to make Muslim communities rise up against Europe. One word sums up the ideal to which we are supposed to submit: oblation. All the duties are on our side, all the rights on that of believers in the Quran, from whom we must conceal even the least luminous aspects of their faith. 'Muslims' ability to make an Islamophobic prejudice recognized and inventoried depends strictly on their ability to establish their own definition and interpretation of their religiousness.'[8] This admission is instructive: 'Muslims' must take control of language and vocabulary in order not to conform to current usage but to dictate their own. They have to be taken as they are. This was proclaimed by the former French minister of justice, the Socialist Christiane Taubira, in a comment that is both paternalistic and revisionist: 'the Arabo-Muslim slave trade must not be mentioned too much so that young Arabs do not bear on their backs all the weight of Arabs' crimes'.[9] Since problems in integrating our Muslim compatriots are all our fault, we have to be hospitable. The 'Other' (but not just any Other, not the Chinese, the Vietnamese, the South American, the Russian, or the Pole, always the Muslim, the only one worthy of acceding to that title of moral nobility) is always right and we are always wrong. Anyway, isn't continental France already a mixture of apartheid and Nazism? In France, it is said, we breathe a sort of atmospheric, consubstantial racism, which takes the form of a constant harassment of people who are different.[10] No peaceful coexistence between human beings, only traps, prejudices, and nastiness that cannot be transcended and that poisons the general climate.[11] As for the Collectif contre l'Islamophobie en France, it denounces 'the crystallization of Islamophobia at the very heart of the Republic's institutions' due to 'secularism', which has been transformed into an 'instrument for stigmatizing and excluding', notably through two laws passed in 2004 and 2010, one that forbids wearing the Islamic veil in schools, and another that forbids wearing the burqa in the public sphere. This racism is thus structural.[12] Above all, France is guilty of being France.

Strangely enough, the exponential growth of Islamophobic acts denounced by many is not confirmed by opinion surveys or by figures. According to the French Interior Ministry's statistics for 2013, anti-religious acts, desecrations of cemeteries and places of worship, injurious statements, and the defacement of façades affect mainly Christians, even if they have increased proportionally for Jews and Muslims in France. The same statistics show a massive increase in anti-Muslim acts in 2015 after the attacks on *Charlie Hebdo*, followed by a spectacular decrease of 54 per cent over the first nine months of 2016.[13] On 3 May 2016, for example, the National Consultative Commission on Human Rights (CNCDH) noted that 'in 2015 the longitudinal index of tolerance in France indicated a clear advance toward more tolerance'. France increasingly sees itself as a plural society. The desire to live together has not diminished, and this is shown notably by an increase in the number of mixed marriages and by the emergence of an elite issuing from diversity.[14] There is, of course, a big gap between individuals' subjective experiences and cold statistics. When surrounded by 'atheists', a very pious person may experience a profound uneasiness that will not be reflected in the statistics. However, faced by terrorist attacks, the French have so far behaved with extraordinary restraint. We have not seen the lynchings and cold-blooded murders of random individuals who wore a turban or had dark skin that occurred in the United States after September 11. French officials have not created a Guantanamo or passed a Patriot Act; they have not invaded Iraq or generalized torture in their armed forces the way George W. Bush's America did. On the whole, our compatriots have behaved in a civilized way, even if a particularly atrocious attack may elicit bloody reprisals and arouse the aggressiveness of small, identitarian groups.[15]

But for the fundamentalists, frictions between Muslims and others must be exaggerated, and every skirmish described in terms of a genuine St Bartholomew's Day massacre. An oblique glance, an ironic smile, suffice to invoke our history's great massacres. In the summer of 2013, the al-Kanz website discovered a case of Islamophobia hidden in the packaging of *Vache qui rit* cheese.[16] For the Committee Against Islamophobia in France (which should be renamed the 'Committee for Islamophobia', so skilled is it in making mountains out of molehills in order to justify its existence), any condemnation of a Salafist preacher inciting hatred of Jews, any measure expelling an individual found guilty of being involved in terrorist activities, is racist.[17] Even the police searches undertaken after a terrorist attack are seen as a humiliation for millions of Muslims; according to the CCIF, they involve subjecting innocent believers to the same treatment given to gangs and hoodlums.[18] In short, defending oneself against terrorists is a racist act! Here we are not far from the crime of collusion with the enemy.

If this reasoning is correct – if the attacks in France, the United States, Germany, and Great Britain are due to the intolerable burden of the vileness of our societies, which are 'allergic to alterity' – then how can we explain the fact that bombings, trucks full of dynamite that cut down hundreds of people in marketplaces, and candidates for suicide attacks are infinitely more numerous in Muslim countries, from Morocco to Indonesia? Is it that these culturally and religiously Islamic countries are also infected by anti-Muslim racism, or rather that Islam itself is being eaten away from inside by the virus of division? Who is Islamophobic if not the extremists of al-Qaeda, ISIS, the al-Nusra Front, Hezbollah, the Muslim Brotherhood, the Taliban, al-Shabaab in Somalia, Hamas, and the Wahhabis, who are killing more Muslims than Westerners will ever kill, and who have made the Prophet's religion a source of fear even for its own believers?

All that is admirable about classic Islamic civilization – the beauty of the Arabic language chanted or recited, the art of gardens, the geometric anticipation of the paradise to come, the symmetry of believers bowed down by an implacable clock at prayer times, the metaphysical vehemence tempered by a culture of compromise and syncretism, in Asia as in Africa,[19] the grace of slender minarets reaching for the sky, the sumptuous calligraphy evading the ban on representation, the divine message's power of attraction, the hospitality and warmth of its believers – all that has been swept away, annihilated over the past thirty years by the abuses perpetrated by Allah's pious mercenaries. The explanation of all this by reference to the West's allergy to alterity is not valid; the goal is simply to delegitimate any questioning of the religion by inventing imaginary connections with Europe's colonial past, even when it is a matter of countries like Sweden, Norway, and Denmark, which had no territorial expansion outside Europe. And if France and its neighbours are so hostile to Islam, how does it happen that Muslim citizens remain there and still want to come there, instead of migrating en masse to milder climes? Isn't it also the constraints of a suffocating piety that they want to escape? The truth is that the advantages they find here surpass any possible tensions.

If for fundamentalists Western culture represents a pathological alterity, Islam, on the contrary, is supposed to incarnate for its believers a 'curative alterity'[20] capable of remedying the malaise and the dead-ends of our civilization. This was expressed in 2006, not without subtlety, by Audalla Conget, an old Cistercian monk of Saragossa who had converted to Islam, in an open letter to Pope Benedict XVI:

> You criticize us in order to conceal your deep admiration for our faith, for our religion full of fervour and perseverance. An unshakeable faith that leads you to ask yourself questions without finding a convincing answer: why do so few Muslims convert to Christianity? And why are there so many of us who, after having been active Christians, now recognize in Islam our place in the universe? If one is a Christian, it is painful to look, every Friday, on mosques full of men and women of all ages, their foreheads pressed against the earth, in the sincerest acceptance of God's will.[21]

It is not certain that today admiration of Islam is as great in a Europe that has been shaken for the past ten years by acts of terror and has witnessed, stunned, the abominable wars that the peoples of the Middle East are waging against each other in the name of the true God. Finally, few Muslims convert to Christianity because they are threatened with death for apostasy if they try to do so. But in a reversal of the practice of the Marranos, many 'Christians *manqués*' conceal their conversion and keep their Muslim first names in order not to tip off those close to them. And this fear extends even to the state. Thus in January 2015, for example, the French Interior Ministry cancelled a certain number of showings of Cheyenne Carron's film *L'Apôtre* (which recounts a young Muslim's conversion to Catholicism while he was preparing to become an imam) in order to avoid 'provoking the Muslim community' and 'the risk of terrorist attacks'. On the other hand, Abd al-Malik's film *Qu'Allah bénisse la France*, released in October

2014, telling the story of a young man brought up Catholic who converts to Islam, has been received as 'a fine lesson of hope and tolerance'. No reciprocity is allowed in this domain.[22] There are mosques in Rome; is there a single church in Riyadh or Mecca?[23]

12

Minorities, Protection or Prison?

> The recognition of every person's humanity has as
> its immediate consequence the recognition of human
> plurality. Humans are beings that speak, but there are
> thousands of languages. Anyone who forgets one of
> these two points falls back into barbarity.
>
> Raymond Aron

On 12 September 2016, the *New York Times* published
on its front page a series of portraits of twelve French,
Dutch, and Belgian women who talked about their
misfortunes connected with being Muslims in countries
where they were insulted, mistreated, and 'looked at'.
One of them explained, for example: 'To be a Muslim
woman in France is to live in an apartheid system of
which the beach bans are just the latest incarnation. ...
I think that French Muslim women would be justified to
request asylum in the United States, for instance, given
how many persecutions we are subjected to.' Another
said: 'I am afraid of having to wear a yellow crescent
on my clothes one day, like the Star of David for Jews
not so long ago.' This report, which is worthy of *Pravda*

at its height, did just one thing wrong: it gave the floor to the prosecution alone, never to the defence, never to the tens of thousands of French Muslim women who are happy to be freed from the veil and the constraints imposed by the Muslim community. How should we understand such an attack on the part of a prestigious press organ? Like anti-Americanism in France, 'French bashing' in the United States has a derivative function. Its goal is to make us forget the murders of dozens of Afro-Americans that the police have recently committed in cold blood, and that remind us of the worst times of segregation; to minimize the activities of supremacist militias that prepare attacks on refugees or migrants; and to erase the calamitous image created by Donald Trump's campaign that was then being conducted.

The *New York Times*, posing as the champion of moral authority, sought to show how superior the British/American system is to French secularism. American democracy was in fact constructed with religions in mind, whereas the French Republic was built on opposition to the monarchy and Catholicism, which it had fought before passing the law separating Church and State in 1905. But the United States, despite the Founding Fathers' indifference in matters of religion – 'Of all the tyrannies that affect mankind, tyranny in religion is the worst', said Thomas Paine – displays a natural good will toward all forms of worship, while atheists and sceptics are the objects of a spontaneous suspicion and even genuine discrimination. Their offence is that they do not form a community, except negatively. The American God is an eclectic and neutral God, made up of all the nations and groups that compose the Republic, a friendly and patriotic entity attentive to the success and well-being of its faithful. In America, religion is plural from the outset; there are hundreds of denominations, with Islam just one among many. (There are 3.3 million Muslims in the United

States, or 1 per cent of the country's population.) This
is in no way comparable to the religious monopoly
that Rome was able to exercise over part of the Old
World, which was later imitated by the Lutheran,
Anglican, and Calvinist Churches. People often contrast
an America that is religious to the point of bigotry to
an agnostic Europe that is supposed to live within a
purely immanent horizon. But America's faith is first of
all a faith in America, the certainty of being a messianic
nation, chosen by Providence to save the world. France,
conversely, sees in secularism the guarantee of freedom
of religion and the equality of religious beliefs. The state
is neutral, and, as John Locke put it, has no legitimacy
when it comes to influencing consciences, or deciding
what is true or false. It is not the owner of spiritual
options; it limits itself to protecting all faiths with
the same equanimity, on condition that none of them
contravenes the Republic's laws or claims to supplant
them. Concretely, French-style secularism is characterized by a long satirical and anti-clerical tradition,
today attenuated, and by the relegation of spiritual
practices to the realm of private life. God must remain
at home, and his partisans must show their enthusiasm
with moderation, without invading the public sphere
for the purpose of proselytizing.

Without seeking to go beyond the framework of this
essay, let us say that there are, roughly speaking, two
kinds of multiculturalism: one of provenance, the other
of destination, even if they can mix. One is a multiculturalism of fact, the other a multiculturalism of value.
The former wants to do justice to the different groups
that make up a society and to protect their particu-
larisms, while the latter stresses less their origin than the
purpose of their presence: the grandeur of the receiving
nation, rich with all these men and women who have
come from diverse countries. That is the meaning of
the pledge of allegiance to the United States, which

makes of each potential citizen, whether they were born in Mexico, Nicaragua, Egypt, Ghana, or Korea, an authentic American thanks to the great melting pot constituted by patriotism and the promise of social advancement. In a France that claims to be a republic, one and indivisible, there is a danger of accumulating the disadvantages of the communitarian model without the advantages of a country sure of itself and its future. The bureaucratic model of 'living together' presupposes the well-behaved alignment of sardines in a can: each community is supposed to coexist with the others, without necessarily encountering them, the state playing the role of justice of the peace and arbitrator.

But a strong nation is never a simple aggregation of individuals who have sprung from different roots: there comes a time when it has to become a fiction that makes sense for everyone and transcends each individual's specificities; a grand narrative that unifies the disparate tribes, which are always in danger of fragmenting. No culture is to be neglected, provided that it respects the fundamental laws and participates in the common momentum. Let us recall that for Plato the great political art consisted in 'weaving' people together, in transforming the heterogeneous human flock into a single people, fabric here being the symbol of civic cohesion. Therefore we must prevent the fabric from being unravelled and its fragile unity from being ripped to shreds. And since humanity exists only in the plural, France, like other European nations, is called upon to exchange the monotony of a homogeneous landscape for multicoloured diversity. But do minorities want to melt into a whole that transcends them, or do they want to remain distinct, to secede from the rest of society? Isn't each of them in danger of degenerating into a micronationalism, demanding special treatment, depending on religion, origins, or skin colour? Should the France of the future remain a grand idea capable of stirring the hearts of millions of people, or should it become a Lego structure that can be taken apart and rebuilt at will? For a community of persons of all colours, of all beliefs, to constitute a society, they have to be united by a great design that is at once collective and individual: patriotism, democracy, the right to fulfil themselves, and the material and moral improvement of their conditions. Without shared values beyond the perimeter of their origins, citizens would be transformed into simple users of a state that has become a mere service provider.

In any case the celebration of differences in sexuality or race cannot serve as the cement holding together a great country. It is characteristic of North America that it remains handicapped by the spirit of segregation, even among adversaries of the establishment. Women's Studies for women, African-American Studies for blacks, Hebrew Studies for Jews, Men's Studies for men, Transgender Studies for the others. Each is urged to stay home and find refuge in the group into which he was born or to which he belongs. It's a kind of house arrest in which one avoids opening one's door to others. And in America electoral campaigns themselves are limited to appealing to blacks, Latinos, gays, whites, one alongside the other in a frenetic clientelism, at the risk of forgetting the common feeling that transcends them all. Minorities are so full of themselves that they can no longer converse with others and prefer to remain among their own kind. As useful as ethnic or gender alliances may be, it is not forbidden to imagine that a Jew might take an interest in African culture, a man in Women's Studies, a heterosexual in homosexuality, or a Christian in Islamic civilization, as so many ways of approaching the universal. Such a 'politics of identity' (Edmund White), pursued on the pretext of restoring the dignity of 'subaltern' groups, can rapidly degenerate into communitarian patriotism. How can a grand idea, the egalitarian coexistence of minorities, turn into a kind of new Balkanization, in the name of tolerance and democracy?

Whereas culture tears us away from our spontaneous ethnocentrism, cultures as traditions are pacifying in so far as they dictate our mode of life and relieve us of the burdens of freedom: thanks to them, life is programmed, choices are simplified, and children will live like their parents, who were already reproducing the acts of their ancestors. The *I* is always a department of the *We*; it confirms a membership more than it announces a dissidence or an innovation. Prejudices, customs, and rituals are more powerful than personal will. But this pacification is also a smothering that dooms us, as Mezri Haddad so precisely put it, to 'perpetual identitarian reclusion'. It is the ambiguity of multiculturalism that it incarcerates men and women in customs from which they often want to free themselves: it postulates a hermetic separation of ways of life that makes them existential prisons. That was recognized by Sadiq Khan, the mayor of London, when he said that 'we have protected people's right to live in accord with their cultural tradition at the expense of living together. Too many British Muslims grow up without really knowing anyone of a different origin.' The politics of identity perpetuates, in the name of anti-racism, the old prejudices attached to race or ethnicity. Each individual evolves in a space-time parallel to that of others without ever actually encountering them.

The possibility of scorning other cultures, Freud wrote, compensates us for the sacrifices we make in order to put up with our own. But if these sacrifices are too great, the temptation is strong to leave one's clan, one's tribe, one's family, in order to set out for other, milder, climes. The protection of minorities' rights includes protecting the right of each individual belonging to these minorities to withdraw from them without damage, by moving away or by forgetting, and to forge his own destiny, far from his own people. It is therefore the right to exist as a private person who cannot be deduced from his roots, and it is also the right, on the religious level, to abandon one's parents' religion, or even to embrace a different one. That is how we should understand republican emancipation: through social promotion and the bracketing of biological and cultural determinisms. *France is detested by fundamentalists not because it oppresses Muslims, but because it frees them.*[1] But the ethnic, religious, or sexual minority sees itself instead as a small nation that has been restored to its original innocence, to which everything is owed because of the wrongs that have been inflicted on it, and in which the most outrageous chauvinism is merely the expression of a legitimate self-regard. All cultures are of equal value but each of them is more valuable than the members who compose it.

As a result, marginal groups have a police that is no less repressive than the usual one. The blackmail used to force people to show ethnic, racial, religious solidarity with and loyalty to the *ummah* serves to reprimand any possible recalcitrants and to restrain their aspirations to freedom. That is why it is so difficult, in Western democracies, to try Muslims in accord with Muslim law, to establish alongside the common law a special law that is often seen by those concerned, especially women, as an abominable regression. Canada, for instance, made an attempt in the province of Ontario, and also in Quebec, to grant religious courts the right to rule on cases involving inheritance and family matters. Women could thereby find themselves driven out of the family home in the event of divorce, lose custody of their children, or receive an inheritance half that accorded their brothers. A Canadian woman of Iranian origin, Homa Arjomand, led the protest to prevent this imposition of Sharia and to allow all citizens, without distinction of sex or religious belief, to remain under the common law.

Multiculturalism, when it comes straight from the source, is perhaps just that: a chosen apartheid in which we hear the unctuous tones of the rich explaining to the poor that money doesn't make you happy: for us, the burdens of freedom, of self-invention, of equality between men and women; for you the joys of custom, forced marriages, the veil, the burkini, polygamy, and clitoridectomy. The members of these small congregations thus become museum pieces, the inhabitants of a reservation that we want to preserve from the calamities of progress. Whereas we could, on the contrary, argue on behalf of fluid memberships, a composite heritage, a multiple personality (like that of France, which is first of all Gallo-Roman and Judeo-Christian, but also Celtic, Central European, Caribbean, Arab, African, Asian). In other words, it is a twofold battle that must be fought: protecting minorities and religions from the discriminations of which they are the objects; and protecting private individuals from the intimidations that their native communities may exercise on them. To adapt a famous formula, in a government of laws, it is the law that protects and custom that oppresses.

13

The Racism of the Anti-Racists

What is this religious culture that periodically provides, on a large scale and over such a long period, whole contingents of people impatient to reach paradise?
                                                                    Hamadi Redissi[1]

In February 1989, when Ayatollah Khomeini issued a *fatwa* against Salman Rushdie calling on every good Muslim to kill him, wherever he might be, for having published *The Satanic Verses* and profaned the image of Muhammad, Rushdie was immediately defended by a majority of intellectuals, including Milan Kundera, Jacques Derrida, Naguib Mahfouz, Mahmoud Darwish, Edward Said, and Pierre Bourdieu. But good apostles had already taken offence at the publication and had only given lip service to the obligation to defend him. President Jacques Chirac declared: 'I do not admire Monsieur Rushdie. I have read what was published in the press. It is deplorable. And in general I have no esteem for those who use blasphemy to make money.'[2] The Canadian philosopher Charles Taylor, who has written on the theory of recognition, and writers as well known as Roald Dahl and John Le Carré, did not conceal their reservations either. The author of *Tinker, Tailor, Soldier, Spy* wrote:

> Rushdie is a victim but in my opinion he is not a hero. I'm sorry for him and I respect his courage [...] but anyone familiar with Muslims [...] knows that anyone who treats the Book [the Quran] lightly does so at his own peril. I believe there is nothing deplorable about religious fervour. American presidents display it in a ritual way and we respect it among Christians and Jews [...] Absolute freedom of expression is not a sacred right in all countries. It is in fact restricted by prejudices, moral perceptions, and decency. No one has the sacred right to insult a great religion and to be published in all impunity.[3]

Fifteen years later, in 2004, Ayaan Hirsi Ali, then a member of the Dutch parliament, was sentenced to death by the fundamentalists for having made, with the filmmaker Theo van Gogh, a film on the condition of women in Islam, *Submission* (van Gogh was assassinated the same year in Holland by a Moroccan extremist, as a kind of punishment). Two famous English-speaking intellectuals, Ian Buruma and Timothy Garton Ash, thereupon accused Hirsi of having 'betrayed' her culture and 'sullied' a minority religion.[4] With the courage of those who attack the weak, they castigated her 'aristocratic style', her 'solemnity', and her 'simplistic ideas', suggesting, like good male chauvinists, that her notoriety derived from her physical attractiveness more than from the cause of women she was defending. Buruma ended up accusing her of having yielded to 'Enlightenment fundamentalism', the Western counterpart of the fundamentalism that commands murders and suicide attacks.

This is a reflex common to defenders of Islamists: they accuse dissidents of being fanatics. Thus, discussing the burkini dispute in August 2016, the

Africanist Jean-François Bayart speaks of the 'Salafists of secularism'.[5] In itself, this expression is meaningless, a mere quip seeking to disqualify anyone whose opinion differs from that of the article's author. Once again, the *New York Times* also resorts to this procedure. In the French prohibition of the burkini on certain beaches, it sees 'a public humiliation and ostracism that recall the moral police of theocratic countries like Iran or Saudi Arabia, not a country that considers its values the paragon of Western freedoms'.[6] Both adversaries are dismissed to demonstrate the moral superiority of the third party who remains above the fray: to fight obscurantism is to be an obscurantist oneself! The Enlightenment, according to Buruma? Nothing other than 'a simple bundle of anthropological prejudices', as Paul Berman acutely sums it up in a virulent criticism of these two intellectuals: 'Ian Buruma and Timothy Garton Ash [...] could no longer reliably tell black from white, a fanatical murderer from a rational debater.'[7]

Practising what I called at the time 'the racism of the anti-racists', Buruma and Garton Ash asked Muslims, and especially women, to bow down before the commandments of their religion and not try to emancipate themselves from them.[8] Making due allowances, these two intellectual sentinels conducted themselves as did the communist fellow-travellers who used to be assigned to denounce the slightest deviant speech coming from the USSR. Another of Islamism's guard dogs, the French university professor Vincent Geisser, was even harsher in castigating Ayaan Hirsi Ali and Irshad Manji, describing them as 'Barbie dolls of Islam-lite' who are defended 'out of the eroticism of victims'.[9]

As time passes, showing irreverence toward Islam and its symbols has become more dangerous for journalists, cartoonists, advertisers, or believers who are opposed to bigots and who know that they are risking physical elimination. The choice is simple: acquiesce or die. Let us recall that the rector of the Islamic Centre in Brussels, Abdullah al-Ahdal, was assassinated in March 1989 for having shown moderation with regard to Salman Rushdie. In addition, Rushdie's Japanese translator was stabbed to death, while his Italian translator and his Norwegian publisher survived attempts to murder them. As for his Turkish translator, while in Sivas for a cultural festival in 1994, he narrowly escaped a fire in the hotel where he was staying, a conflagration in which thirty-seven people died. In 1989 copies of the sacrilegious book were publicly burned in the British city of Bradford, in an auto-da-fé worthy of that in Nuremberg in 1933.

The insolence required by the 'subversive' left flips over into prostration. For the 'Parti collabo', it is better to accuse those who revolt against terrorism than to join them. The holy alliance of fear and the Crescent does wonders when it comes to shutting people's mouths and dictating calming remarks to rebellious authors. Whence the contortions of intellectuals and scholars who ignore any protest within Islam to avoid putting themselves in danger. It is precisely that cowardice that Salman Rushdie (the *fatwa* issued against him is still running, and the reward has now risen to 3.6 million dollars) deplored in attacking North American writers who refused, out of 'anti-racism', to join in the PEN club's ceremony held in April 2015 in honour of the victims at *Charlie Hebdo* (among these writers: Michael Ondaatje, Joyce Carol Oates, Teju Cole, Russell Banks, Francine Prose, and Peter Camp, formerly tutelary figures of the American left). And while two very popular French rappers, Kol Shen and Akhenaton, 'the moral consciences of their generation',[10] demanded an 'auto-da-fé for those curs at *Charlie Hebdo*',[11] two other figures of the French intelligentsia demanded in turn nothing less than a severe restriction of the right to free expression: the day after the killings at *Charlie Hebdo*, the far-left philosopher Étienne Balibar wrote that the cartoons published by this magazine showed an 'indifference to the possibly disastrous consequences of a healthy provocation: in this case, the humiliation felt by millions of people who have already been stigmatized, which makes them susceptible to the manipulations of organized fanatics'.[12] As for the sociologist Edgar Morin, he argued for the more or less tacit prohibition of blasphemy. 'Must we allow freedom to offend the faith of believers in Islam by degrading the image of its prophet?'[13] Out of cowardice or paternalism, censorship has won in Europe: we will no longer see images of Muhammad in any newspaper or magazine; Voltaire's play *Mahomet ou le fanatisme* (written, moreover, in 1736 against the Catholic Church and the French monarchy) will no longer be performed; mockeries, insolences, and bawdy remarks are henceforth forbidden so far as Islam is concerned.[14] The crime of lèse-divinity is supported by part of the left and by Christian conservatives in the name of respect for convictions.

It is true that we must protect cultures and religions, but on two conditions: that they situate themselves within the framework of the common law, and do not seek exorbitant prerogatives with regard to the law. That is why we cannot agree that Muslim girls should be exempt from classes in gymnastics, from swimming pools, or the beach on the grounds that their religion forbids them, or that halal cafeterias should be introduced in schools or offices (even if we should, of course, continue to offer substitute meals). We cannot allow 'religious' men, in offices or elsewhere, to refuse to shake women's hands for fear of being polluted by the contact. Or allow women to be forbidden to go to cafés, as they are in certain predominantly Muslim areas near Paris.[15] We cannot tolerate seeing a doctor forbidden to examine a Muslim woman because he is a man, or a ramp agent at Roissy airport refuse to guide an Air France plane that has just landed, on the grounds that the captain on board is a woman.[16] We cannot accept that a young woman's family can force her to marry an uncle or a cousin in her village whom she does not love, or that a husband can seek a divorce on the grounds that the merchandise was misrepresented because the bride was not a virgin on her wedding night and lied about her essential qualities, as happened in the Lille district court on 1 April 2008 (the decision was subsequently overturned by the appellate court in Douai in November of the same year). Finally, we cannot show the slightest indulgence for crimes of honour that lead a brother or a father to kill their sister or daughter on the grounds that she is supposed to have dishonoured her family by living in the Western style. The right to practise one's religion does not involve exemption from the rules of common life. If in a secular regime the state's function is to guarantee religious diversity, its mission is also, as we have said, to place all citizens under the protection of the law and to safeguard them against the dictates of the community to which they belong. Having emerged from the old colonialist law, multiculturalism, in a dizzying reversal, has thus returned from the left: now each human being is supposed to be a prisoner of the conditions under which he was born, bound to his religion, which has become, like the colour of his skin, an insuperable barrier. An excellent example of this reversal: the speech given by Barack Obama in Cairo on 4 June 2009, in which, hoping to pacify Islam in general, he defended the veil for women, that is, official segregation.[17] He did so again in a mosque in Baltimore in 2016 when he congratulated an African-American woman fencer, Ibtihaj Muhammad, for having the courage to compete in the Olympic Games wearing an Islamic scarf and to show her convictions against intolerance and hatred. His attitude was all the more surprising because Michelle Obama, visiting Saudi Arabia with her husband in 2009, had refused to wear the veil. A year later, she was imitated by Princess Mary of Denmark, to the great dismay of Saudi Arabia's elite. What is authorized for a First Lady or a princess is not authorized for ordinary citizens? It is after all strange that the president of the United States never says a word about the Muslim women in Iran, Iraq, or elsewhere who want to take off their scarves or burn them in public as a symbol of oppression (forgetting that the unveiling begun at the end of the nineteenth century in Egypt, Turkey, Tunisia, and Morocco, the rejection of claustration for women, was carried out by the great modernizers, from Ataturk to Bourguiba);[18] or about the female Kurdish soldiers in Iraq and Syria who are proud to fight with their heads uncovered and for whom being a soldier is a token of advancement and emancipation.[19]

To all the lovers of the Islamic veil, we must suggest that it be extended to men: why should a male's hair be less immodest than that of a young woman? Is woman by nature an impure entity who must hide her head and her face? You want the hijab: but then for both sexes, from puberty onward! You men defend the burkini? Then why not a male equivalent, 'burxers', as the former *Charlie Hebdo* cartoonist Zineb el Rhazoui humorously suggested?[20] Absolute equality! The reader may recall that in Mecca in 2002 committees for the protection of virtue prevented some fifteen girls from leaving a school on fire because they had taken off their veils to escape the building. They all died, but the dogma was safe. The burkini affair in the summer of 2016 was obviously a trap laid for the French authorities: it is not easy for the constabulary to dictate to women the way they should dress or undress, and the fundamentalists' ploy succeeded perfectly. The matter should have been handled with humour, charm, and counter-provocation, not by force; for example, by sending brigades of women in G-strings, bikinis, or topless to mix with the others, in order to goad them into making trouble. Once accepted, the veil or the burqa threatens to become the norm for all Muslim women, distinguishing the modest from the indecent and penalizing those who refuse to wear them. *It is the perversity of obscurantism that it makes freedom appear to be an anomaly and enslavement a norm.* How can we not see that the burqa (or the niqab), for example, apart from the fact that it wraps the body in a shroud, is the racist uniform par excellence because it says to everyone: you are not worthy of looking at me, your eyes sully my nature as a superior being. Many European countries, including Germany, are considering prohibiting it; they will inevitably do so, for reasons of security. If Islam is to be saved, it will be saved by women, who are everywhere enslaved, restricted, supervised, second-class citizens, and they have everything to gain by demanding a better status.

The debate about multiculturalism proves that the limitless praise of 'distinctive characters' and 'traditions' can conceal the same twisted paternalism that was once practised by the colonizers. To each his own barbarity, as it were. People don't care how others live and suffer once they have been parked in the ghetto of their inviolable particularity. We believe, for instance, that we are purchasing social peace at the price of 'reasonable accommodations', a little like the mayors of problem areas who close their eyes to the practices of radical imams out of clientelism or in order to win votes when election time rolls around. To refuse to ask our Muslim compatriots to respect the same rights and duties that other citizens are required to respect – Protestants, Catholics, Orthodox Jews, Hindus, or agnostics – is quite simply to refuse them equality.

A certain liberalism is based on the hypothesis that equal citizens can peacefully cohabit in the same space, despite their different views of the sovereign good, provided that they agree on a limited number of basic principles. Each individual does what he pleases without the public authority interfering in individual choices, but the juxtaposition of incompatible ways of life seems possible only on paper. The open society is not a society open to everything. Tolerance has its limits, especially when applied to insular groups closed to any evolution, hostile to any compromise, and who decide for themselves what is just and what is unjust, what is licit and what is illicit. We cannot align radically different worldviews without becoming incoherent. In practice, if women in burkinis and women in bikinis or topless, or even full nudists, are on the same beach, the first group will revolt and end up driving away the others. Similarly, a restaurant will have to separate customers who drink alcohol from those for whom drinking fermented beverages is a sin, and who will not put up with even seeing a bottle of wine on a neighbouring table. Picnics in the countryside will also be subjected to the same rule, with drinkers of beer or champagne, like pork-eaters, having to hide themselves to avoid upsetting the pure and the bigots. Finally, when the Islamic veil has become the rule because it has spread like a plague from San Francisco to Moscow, from Rabat to the Sunda Islands, from Stockholm to Cape Hope, it is women with their heads uncovered who will seem strange and need to be re-educated. In some French cities, virtue squads are already tracking down women dressed in shorts and leggings. Determined minorities will always win out over hesitant majorities, wrapping their religious blackmail in a liberal flag. The usual nonsense: we think that to assimilate foreign groups we have to show tolerance, openness, and generosity, and mute our own personalities. If we are nice to them, they will be nice to us. But what if it's the other way around? What if we have to begin by drawing strict limits, showing respect for our fundamental principles, and asking newcomers to share the way of life that flows from these principles? As liberal as it seeks to be, multicultural America still offends the fundamentalists too much: San Bernardino, Orlando, New Jersey, New York – to mention only the attacks in 2016 – show that it is its very existence that offends the bigots. Whatever its good will, the United States remains detested in the vast majority of the Muslim world, and its 'allies' are not the least virulent in this animosity: the United States is hated both for intervening haphazardly, as in Iraq in 2003, and for not intervening, for being an inconsistent sheriff. Whatever it does, it's never enough, or it's too much. In addition, it has the defect of surviving its failures and retaining an insolent pre-eminence, despite resounding bankruptcies. Wasn't it Sayyid Qutb, the ideologist of the Muslim Brotherhood (hanged by Nasser in 1966) and the great thinker of radical Islam, who conceived a fierce aversion to the West in 1948, after spending time in the United States, that nation of opulence and indecency whose freedom of mores, materialism, and loss of soul horrified him?[21] 'The hideous schizophrenia' of the modern world, divided between science and belief, reason and divine aspiration, crowned his disgust.

Once our civilization has been designated as Satanic, nothing can calm the fury of doctrinarians. And nothing equals the blindness of liberals confronted by the doctrinarians' exterminating will. Liberals don't believe in evil, only in misunderstandings. We don't choose our enemies. It is the latter who subject us to their condemnation, whether we want it or not. And they will persist in hating us even if we insist on our good will. That is why we have to take them seriously and especially believe what they say. They will do what they say and say what they will do. That is the minimal politeness we owe them. That does not mean that we respect them. It is true that Saladin (1138–93) aroused boundless admiration among the Crusaders because he waged (and won) wars in a humane and chivalrous manner, even though his adversaries did not.[22] And Emir Abdelkader (1808–83), a redoubtable military leader and a symbol of the battle against French colonization in Algeria, was described as a genius and a 'modern Jugurtha' by General Bugeaud and later considered a friend of France: exiled to Damascus and pensioned by Napoleon III, in 1860 he protected thousands of Christians against the Druses, thereby risking his own life. He was rewarded with the Great Cross of the Legion of Honour and with various marks of recognition on the part of the pope, the czar, and the king of Prussia. But the jihadists in no way deserve our esteem: they do not fight, they commit suicide while killing as many people as possible. These slovenly Nazis are mercenaries of death, zombies without law but not without faith, even if it is a faith led astray by nihilism.

14

Should the West be Decolonized?

> The hand trembles when it comes to the crimes committed by the Arabs, whereas the inventory of the crimes committed by Europeans rightly occupies whole pages.
>
> Marc Ferro (1992)[1]

Decolonization is an illusion: it has not taken place. If we accept the standard opinion, today we are experiencing in France a situation analogous to that of the 1920s, when Paris controlled territories on four continents. This taboo must be broken immediately: it is the 'colonial fracture'[2] that is supposed to explain the fragile, marginalized situation of the children of black and North African immigrants, to whom the schemas used in the ex-Empire continue to be applied. According to Pascal Blanchard, the North Africans fall back on religion because France rejects them.[3] On the other hand, the 'Appel des indigènes' issued by several associations during the winter of 2005 declared that 'Our parents and grandparents were enslaved [...] as sons and daughters of immigrants, we are [...] engaged in the battle against the oppression and discrimination produced by the post-colonial republic [...] we have to put an end to institutions that reduce groups issuing from colonization to the status of subhumans.' One of the authors of this appeal, Sadri Khiari, who defines himself as a native 'non-white', and who is concerned to emphasize the links between colonialism and racism, hopes one day 'to integrate gypsies into the de-colonial dynamics that is emerging' in the immigrant housing projects.[4] On 21 June 2010, a petition launched in *Libération* and signed by Éric Hazan, Antoine Volodine, Siné, Rokhaya Diallo, and others denounced the police, who had allegedly provoked 'kids' in the projects in Villiers-le-Bel, one of the suburbs on the east side of Paris, to fire on them. It described the police as 'occupation forces' at war with the people, necessarily caricatured as a group of 'polygamous delinquents with wives in burqas'.

For his part, Benjamin Stora, an expert on North Africa, explains that France still does not want to confront its colonial past in Algeria – despite over 3,000 books having been published on the subject (belatedly, to be sure), along with about fifty fiction films and around thirty documentaries.[5] As for immigration, it is unavoidable and indispensable, as a 'group of eminent figures' (Joschka Fischer, Javier Solana, Timothy Garton Ash) said in 2011, because it compensates for Europe's demographic deficit. Others maintain that immigration is the price to be paid for colonization and the slave trade, and it will lead to a change in the population, whether we want it or not. The Third World movement, inaugurated at Bandung in the 1950s, must be continued until it effects a metamorphosis of the nations that carried out the imperialist enterprise. These nations deserve only one fate: pure and simple dilution by being inundated with foreigners. The conclusion: the old France, nauseating and rancid, must disappear, because it is still branded by its criminal past. Europe's only vocation is to become a host for everyone and to disappear as a white, Judeo-Christian entity.

Social problems are supposed to be first of all ethnic problems, and immigrant neighbourhoods nothing other than our new 'dominions'. Paris is supposed to be taking over the projects, exploiting their riches, conducting a violent policy of despoliation! Let us recall that others have sought to make the suburbs the equivalent of the occupied territories in Palestine, a Gaza Strip and a West Bank all their own, around Lyon, Toulouse, and Marseille. So here the French are becoming a colonized people in their home country, and they have to be dispossessed of it. Instead of admitting that the French system discourages initiative, that an unemployment rate of 40 per cent among young people in the projects, the lack of skills, and the omnipresence of gangs makes their situation catastrophic, people invent an imaginary genealogy, and the immigrant suburbs are seen through the lens of the conflicts in Algeria and on the high plateaus of Vietnam. Here we are in a kind of spatio-temporal telescoping: periods and continents are superimposed, Seine-Saint-Denis and Aleppo, Clichy and Gaza, Bobigny and the slave trade. Depending on their inclinations, each individual can inhabit the virtual land of slavery and colonialism, which have become vague concepts, temporary habitats that people move into in order to express their anger and frustration. But the situation in the immigrant suburbs is a matter of rejection, of spatial separation, not of the subordination to commercial goals that was the essence of empires. Colonists occupied a country, they didn't abandon it, didn't make it a 'lost territory of the republic'.[6]

Post-colonial studies that are content to repeat without originality the classic anti-imperialist discourse are of limited value; in addition, in order to justify themselves they have to postulate that the West is still the world's master, which it hasn't been for a long time. To tell the truth, the trial of colonialism has been reopened, not because it has been ignored in the schools, but because it provides clarity for those who long for the old divisions. A whole generation of Third-Worldists who miss the old battles are resuming the liberation struggles half a century after independence was won, mumbling in a senile way the catechism of the 1950s and 1960s. For a significant portion of the intelligentsia, talking about colonialism is a way of mourning the revolutionary romanticism and political energy of that time. We can understand why many historians also use the term to exploit a juicy stock-in-trade; nonetheless, the expression 'post-colonial' includes one word too many: it is post- because the point is to say that nothing has changed (it is possible that the post-colonial will last longer, as an academic discipline, than colonialism itself). World history is supposed to recount the immemorial conflict between a white master and a native, a modern-day Spartacus. A single drama with different actors. Confronted by these academic rantings, how can we not think of those Japanese soldiers lost on islands in the Pacific where they continued the Second World War decades after the emperor had surrendered in 1945?

Half a century after decolonization, anti-colonialism is the presentable outer garment of progressivism's unemployed soldiers. What wouldn't they do to adorn themselves with this glorious old cast-off? One example among others: the movie director Christophe Honoré, producing Mozart's opera *Cosi fan tutte* in Aix-en-Provence in June 2016, transposed the action to Ethiopia under occupation by Mussolini's Italy. By doing so he sought to denounce colonialism and fascism. The connection is not clear; so far as I know, Mozart was not interested in Africa, and *Cosi fan tutte* is a comedy about the game of love and infidelity. Above all, we see that the gentleman in question wants to strike the pose of a great world conscience and act out the 'politically committed left'. According to certain academics, internal colonial domination works all the better because it doesn't need to express itself. It is an unconscious mechanism that seems to be taken for granted. 'Colonial fracture': this term, as vague as anyone could wish, makes it possible to explain just about anything, and draws its power from its false simplicity. Does it mean that France is still marked by its recent history? That is to state the obvious. That immigrants from our former colonies are mistreated, relegated to subaltern tasks? That employers and public authorities dream of importing them when they need them and deporting them when jobs are in short supply? That's right – as in almost all European countries, even those that have no imperial past. Are these migrants from North Africa or sub-Saharan Africa less well treated than Tamils, Pakistanis, Sinhalese, Filipinos, or even people from the Baltic states, Poles, Romanians, and Ukrainians, all nationalities of countries that we have not occupied? Wasn't it the Poles who were subjected, after the Brexit vote in the United Kingdom, to a violent xenophobia that went even so far as murder?

The fact that the French labour market remains closed to foreigners does not have to do with a colonial position but rather with a Malthusian logic: in France, parties of both the right and the left chose, as early as the 1980s, to tolerate structural unemployment in order to protect certain categories of unionized workers or officials, at the price of dooming the younger generations to idleness or low-paid jobs. The fact that France is stagnant on the economic level, that it exhausts the middle classes with exorbitant taxation, that its public expenditure (at 57.5 per cent) is unequalled in Europe, and that it has an unemployment rate of more than 10 per cent, is not proof of colonialism but of sheer incompetence, especially when it is compared with its great neighbour, Germany. Finally, the peri-urban groups studied by the geographer Christophe Guilluy, who feel abandoned by the welfare state and the media in favour of the livelier suburbs, are also badly off. France has failed, but it has failed for all its citizens, not only for immigrants. Colonialism has become a portmanteau word that no longer designates a precise historical process but rather everything that the various lobbies, and especially that of the Islamists, challenge in France: the republican ideal, secularism, and the equality of men and women, but also the country's economic failure.

One hates to have to remind people of this obvious fact: decolonization took place. It is no doubt very imperfect and has left traces, but France has finally turned over a new page. If it wants to move beyond this period, that is because in this area the consequence of detachment is amnesia. For example, Algeria is no longer a French passion, outside the limited circle of the repatriates, whereas France remains an Algerian passion. What moves French groups is more than ever the memory of the two world wars, the humiliation of the defeat in 1940, and the stain of collaboration, from which we have still not recovered. The speed with which in the 1960s continental France resigned itself to the loss of its empire, forgetting along the way a few hundred thousand *pieds-noirs* and *harkis*,[7] proves that the colonial enterprise was probably not as dear to the hearts of the French as people say it was.

It is true that we have to reconstruct our colonial memories, just as we have done for other periods. But if it is a question of a memory, that is because the events are in the past. In 1962, it might have been right to speak of the considerable impact of the loss of the empire and of the narcissistic wound that followed from it (Benjamin Stora), but that is no longer the case.

What 'narcissistic wound', by the way? It was a relief to be rid of the empire; nobody wanted to die for Algeria or Morocco when the revolution in mores and the construction of Europe were beginning! Seen from our present perspective, and even if the battle for Algerian independence almost provoked a civil war in France, the conquest of Algeria in 1830 and then the struggle to keep it in the French community, even at the price of coercion, seems an aberration from another age. What were we doing there, anyway? It's an understatement to say that we disapprove, we have moved on. A nation is made great not by its territorial conquests but by its spiritual and scientific advances. Contemporary France no longer dreams of imperialism; it is fed by a patriotism of retraction and not of expansion, it dreams of closing its frontiers rather than infinitely expanding them. Today, its true motto is instead 'down with the outside world'.

A great power is always better off recognizing its crimes and asking forgiveness for them, even if it is not certain that such a step will calm resentments. It is Europe's honour to confess its crimes and to teach them; many states refuse to revisit the past (like present-day Turkey with regard to the Armenian genocide, for example). The Old World is one of the few continents that has been able to think through its barbarity and to distance itself from it. History is not divided into sinful countries and archangel continents, accursed races and untouchable peoples; the division is between democracies that confess their faults, and dictatorships, whether secular or theocratic, that conceal them by clothing themselves in martyrs' rags. No people is innocent or guilty a priori. Over the past sixty years, many decolonized countries have proven that they are as capable as we are of committing abominations, invading and pillaging their neighbours, imprisoning their opposition, liquidating dissenters, impoverishing their populations. To avoid having to question themselves, they adopt the posture of the victim and continue to blame their errors on the former colonialist countries. We owe them everything because of the suffering they have endured. But instead of admitting their mistakes and confronting them directly, they seek in their earlier oppression excuses for their present malfeasance. Thus Algerians have long demanded that France apologize before signing a friendship treaty. Why not admit publicly the reality of 'the dirty war', the use of torture, the brutality of colonization in that country? But the Algerians need to be urged to do the same, to reveal their shadowy sides, to clean up at home. A politics of contrition always demands a certain reciprocity.

To talk constantly about neo-colonialism is to strengthen the prejudices that one seeks to extirpate; one can no longer consider the Other as an equal but only as a perpetually oppressed victim, locked up in his skin, his origins. In the end, this amounts to denying change in history, to confusing the rupture with its sequels. One has to feel very sure of oneself in order to say – as the president of the People's Republic of China did when he welcomed Margaret Thatcher in 1985 – 'The British occupation awoke China from its age-old slumbers'; or to emphasize – as did the former prime minister of India, Manmohan Singh, on receiving an honorary doctorate from Oxford in July 2005 – the positive aspects of the British Empire, which India was certainly justified in combating but from which it also drew 'beneficial consequences'. These great powers, masters of their destiny, not only acquired their independence but emerged from the post-colonial era, the final bond of subjection. They finally reached maturity.

Part V

What is God's Future?

Our God who art in heaven, stay there.

Jacques Prévert

15

Is the War on Terror a Sham?

The Quran is our constitution. Jihad is our path, dying on Allah's path is our greatest hope.

Motto of the Muslim Brotherhood

'Viva la muerte' ('Long live Death!') and 'Death to intelligence!'[1]

Rallying cries of Franco's supporters during the Spanish Civil War (1936–9)

On 28 December 2014, the president of Egypt, Abdel Fattah el-Sisi, gave a formal address before the imams of Al-Azhar University, a bastion of Sunni Islam. He had been re-elected with almost 95 per cent of the vote after he had overthrown, in a coup d'état during the summer of 2013, Mohamed Morsi, the head of the Muslim Brotherhood, and begun a ruthless repression of the latter's supporters. He explained to his audience that the fears aroused by Islam in the world are not without foundation and proceed especially from Islam itself: 'this corpus of texts and ideas, which over many years we have sacralised to the point that departing from it has become almost impossible, arouses the whole world's hostility toward us'. Then he asked this terrible question: 'is it conceivable that one billion six hundred million persons can think that they must kill the other seven billion members of the human race in order to live only among themselves?' Addressing the preachers, scholars, and the grand mufti Ahmed el-Tayeb, the sheikh of Al-Azhar, he asked them to revolutionize their religion that had become infected by ideology, because 'the whole Islamic nation is being torn apart, destroyed, and is on the road to ruin'. Marshal el-Sisi was not the first head of state to make this observation: in Bali on 13 May 2006, opening a summit for a more prosperous Muslim world, the then president of Indonesia, Susilo Bambang Yudhoyono, after pointing out that Muslims had been the first globalizers, noted sadly that among the nations adhering in varying degrees to Islam, 'there is not one that can be classified as developed according to any criterion. All of them are behind in knowledge, finances, and technologies [...] The world associates Islam with backwardness. This makes us angry, but the fact remains that we are backward. We are dependent on others for everything connected with our vital needs [...] nothing in our religion tells us that we cannot be developed.' And again, the Algerian writer Boualem Sansal observes: 'in fourteen centuries, no attempted revolution in ideas comparable to that of the Enlightenment has emerged or taken shape in the Muslim universe'.[2] Islam is sick, according to the reformers of the nineteenth-century *nahda* (renaissance), notably the Syrian Abdraham Kawakbi (1845–1902) and the Syrian-Lebanese emir Chakib Arslan (1869–1946), a diagnosis that fundamentalism was later to turn to its own advantage.[3]

What can we learn from these observations made many years apart? That the Islamic world, behind an appearance of aggressiveness, is in the process of committing suicide in a spiral of violence and chaos. That the unhealthy fascination it exercises on people's minds is that of an imminent apocalypse. And finally, that since it has been the object of a theological hold-up by the Wahhabis, Islam has unfortunately become the favoured reference point for all the unbalanced assassins, hoodlums, and lost soldiers of the world who invoke it with delight and appeal to it in order to justify killing. Let us recall that Sunnism's highest authority, Al-Azhar University in Cairo, waited until the end of 2014, when a Jordanian pilot was burned alive in a cage, to condemn the leaders of ISIS and agree that they might not be good Muslims![4] When Olivier Roy, by simply inverting the genitive, proclaims that we are seeing 'an Islamization of radicality and not a radicalization of Islam', he exempts, in a clever pirouette, the Quranic religion from any examination, and seems to deny that this phenomenon has any religious dimension. If radicality is being Islamized, that is because Islam, and not Buddhism or Hinduism, offers a propitious soil for it. Gilles Kepel, who speaks Arabic and prefers investigative fieldwork to speculation at his desk, seems more convincing when he places the hegemony of the Salafist discourse at the heart of the terrorist plan of action.[5] On the political market, radical Islam offers, thirty years after the fall of the Berlin Wall, the only worldwide alternative, accompanied by a transcendent dimension: mass murder with a divine face, salvation through martyrdom. Better than any other movement, it symbolizes sacrificial extravagance: the imaginary return to the luminous origins, along with the promise of instant accession to paradise. How can such seductiveness be resisted, especially at a time of life, adolescence, that is the age of the Absolute (one sees few jihadists over fifty)?

The war on terrorism is both an absolute necessity and a delusion. While we confront the jihadists, the

Salafists, Wahhabis, and Muslim Brothers advance their pawns, impose their views and clothing customs, multiply their provocations, splinter middle-of-the-road Islam, and push moderate imams aside. They are winning the semantic battle and the war for people's minds. Political Islam is winning: thirty-seven years after the Iranian Revolution, it is flying its flags everywhere, spreading its customs and conquering the hearts of a majority of believers. It runs through all families and those who disapprove of it do not dare to denounce it. Even European Muslims vote for it.[6] Such is the consequence of the pact between the Arab Muslim autocrats, whether secular or not, and the fundamentalists: we'll handle the secular power, you handle religious affairs!

In this sense the two weapons of terror and preaching, one military, the other political, go hand in hand and pursue the same objective: the re-Islamization of the *ummah*, then the Islamization of Europe, the United States, and the whole infidel world.[7] Consider someone like Tariq Ramadan: he sees Islam as the sole alternative that can be opposed to a world corrupted by capitalism and the new economic order: 'The only ones left, it seems, are the implacable ones, the Muslims.'[8] The integration of Muslims in Europe? 'Islam is a factor that needs to be taken into account and will need to be in the future. If this reality continues to be denied, it will inevitably produce radical resistance and clashes.'[9] In other words, it is for Muslims to impose their conditions on the various societies in which they are minorities. If the latter deny them the veil, the burqa, segregated swimming pools and beaches, special Sharia courts, places for prayer in businesses, or halal food in prisons and schools, there will be attacks, massacres. It's secession or punishment. The suicide bombers are the fundamentalists' vanguard, preparing the ground by means of bombs and murder. 'Islam has twice entered Europe and twice left it. Maybe the next conquest will take place, Allah willing, through preaching and ideology. Not all land is necessarily conquered by the sword ... we want an army of preachers and teachers to present Islam in all languages and all dialects' (Yusuf al-Qaradawi, a Muslim Brotherhood theologian who has taken refuge in Qatar and preaches on Al Jazeera).

Terrorism and fundamentalism are twin brothers that act by different means. In this sense, the jihadists are the legislators of the *fait accompli*. Each time they set thresholds of tolerance that stun people, awakening a vocation in some, dread in others. Now, unless there are at least a few dozen deaths, we shrug our shoulders. Tragically, we have become used to this. *Each crime constitutes a law.* If a school is attacked by the Taliban in Pakistan, the same might happen tomorrow in England or in Australia. There are no longer any borders or any taboos. Extortion is based on the spirit of escalation. One has to do better and more than the preceding 'brothers'. What has taken place can always be surpassed by another, even more atrocious, killing spree. Terror rehabilitates a much-decried pathology: paranoia. The most horrifying hypothesis is the most plausible. It obliges us to conceive everything in terms of the worst-case scenario. Jihad is the 'death industry', Hassan al-Banna, the founder of the Muslim Brotherhood, warned in 1937, but it is death put in the service of an infinitely noble goal, the great return to the original caliphate, to the time of the Prophet. The mental universe of the seventh century combined with the hyper-technology of the twenty-first century. Islam's most striking contribution to civilization is the explosive belt and mass slaughter by individuals wearing Nikes and GoPro cameras.

Is the difference between Islam and Islamism a difference of nature or degree? A chasm or a simple slope? After each attack, we see an increased number of self-proclaimed 'experts' who assure us, with a knowing air, that this is not the true Islam.[10] We would like to believe them, but if by some misfortune sectarian Islam became the majority Islam, the distinction would be difficult to maintain. 'The religion of peace' would seem to have been led astray by criminal zealots, becoming the religion of the peace of cemeteries. The whole difficulty, as we know, is that the holy Book is supposed to be 'uncreated', the fruit of a 'divine dictation', whereas the Christian gospels, for example, were written by Christ's disciples. In the Quran, everything is to be taken literally, and thus commentary is forbidden. How could the profane dare to interpret a text that is sacred by nature, how could they dare to soil it by changing even a comma? In this regard, let us salute the speech given by Mohammed VI in Tangier on 21 August 2016. The king of Morocco, who is the Commander of the Faithful and a descendant of the Prophet, set out to sever the link between the Quran and the extremists. Addressing the Moroccan diaspora tempted by jihadism in Europe and in the Middle East, he expressed his horror at the recent murders committed in France and especially that of Father Hamel, who was killed in his church at Saint-Étienne-du-Rouvray:

> The terrorists who act in the name of Islam are not Muslims and their only connection with Islam is the excuses they proudly assert to justify their crimes and their insanities. They are lost individuals doomed to Hell forever. Ignorance leads them to believe that their actions are connected with jihad. But since when does jihad involve killing innocent people? [...] Is it conceivable that God, the All-clement, the All-merciful, could order an individual to blow himself up or to kill innocent people? Yet Islam, as we know, does not authorize any form of suicide, for any reason whatever, as is attested in the verse that says: 'whoso kills a soul, unless it be for murder or for wreaking corruption in the land, it shall be as if he had killed all mankind'.

In Islam, jihad is subject to rigorous conditions: it can be envisaged only as necessary self-defence, and not to commit a murder or aggression [...] Those who incite to murder and aggression, who unduly excommunicate people and interpret the Quran and the Sunna in conformity with their interests, are simply spreading lies in the name of God and the Prophet. That is the true unbelief, as God's word attests [...], as is confirmed by the Hadith of our ancestor, the Prophet, peace and salvation be upon him: 'Whoever tells lies about me deliberately, let him take his place in Hell.'[11]

Islam, which no one worried about before the 1979 Iranian Revolution, has since become an obsessive concern. Few religions have benefited as much from such indulgence and curiosity for almost forty years. Obviously, not all Muslims are terrorists, but all terrorists claim to be authentic Muslims, staining the reputation of their co-religionists and creating a terrible confusion. Whence the necessity of regenerating that great religion through critical, exegetical thought, of historicizing the Quran instead of essentializing it, of purging it of the verses hostile to Jews, Christians, polytheists, and infidels, and of proscribing the barbarous customs of lapidation and repudiation.

That is the project that concerns the whole of humanity: we have to make Islam ordinary, make it a religion among others, not the other of all religions.

Although timid reactions are beginning to appear after every attack, and although intellectual and religious leaders may speak out courageously, European Islam must abandon its passivity toward extremists. In the aftermath of the killings, we are still waiting to see the great demonstrations of believers like those that took place after the affair of the cartoons in *Charlie Hebdo* in 2006, or those that appear every time there is a confrontation between Israel and Hamas.[12] There is a schizophrenia, and almost a tragedy, that afflicts so-called moderate Muslims in Europe: they are called upon, paradoxically, to remain discreet but also to demonstrate noisily in order to distinguish themselves from terrorists or fundamentalists. They are supposed to tell their co-religionists, loudly and clearly, to show restraint in the exercise of their faith. We expect them to report their neighbours or family members and friends who have become radicalized, and ask women who are wholly veiled to show their faces. We would like them to leave their community, but if they defend an Enlightenment Islam, we mock their naivety. In this conflict of loyalties, they are in danger of losing on all levels: too Muslim for society, which suspects them of doublespeak; not Muslim enough for their family and friends, who accuse them of having gone over to the enemy. They are pushed back into the world of shadows and dogmatism from which they are trying to escape. That is the tragically uncomfortable position inhabited by all the great deserters since Salman Rushdie – death threats and a twofold excommunication that plunges them into an extreme solitude. Worse yet: instead of celebrating them as allies, we see them as trouble-makers, accusing them of creating problems for us with majority Islam. In any event, they're in the wrong.

What we owe to the Prophet's religion is not pity for its fate but the truth: the recognition of its past grandeur, its current tragedy, and the urgency of its transformation. Fundamentalism wants to make life impossible for Muslims in order to make them rise up against the 'infidels' and draw every European country into a civil war. For several generations, terrorism has besmirched the Quranic religion's face, soiled with blood all its symbols – the veil, the hijab, the beard – and even transformed the confession of faith: *Allahu Akbar* has become a cry as sinister as the Nazis' *Sieg Heil*. By trying to conquer the world, fundamentalism has attracted its hostility. Just as Catholicism made itself odious for several centuries after the Inquisition, the witch-hunts, the St Bartholomew's Day massacre, and burning people at the stake in the Middle Ages. Because of the jihadists' evil deeds, it has been possible for Donald Trump to demand the closure of the United States' borders to Muslims coming from dangerous countries, and Geert Wilders to demand that the Quran be prohibited in Holland and that mosques be closed. (In this regard, let us note the astonishing harmony between the far right and a certain gay movement that is exasperated by the fate Islamo-fascists plan for homosexuals. It is true that the cult book of so-called 'quietist' Salafism, Aboubaker Djaber Eldjazaïri's *La Voie du Musulman*, justifies slavery, and recommends beating wives and punishing homosexuals.)[13] *We may be afraid of Islam; we may also be afraid for Islam, which will become even fiercer as it declines.* The religion that is 'coming back' is not the great historical Islam, but a mortally wounded religion, unless it is torn out of Wahhabism's lethal grip. Certainties are exasperated when they collapse, and it is then that a religion shows its most hideous face. The fact that in Iran civil society is detaching itself from the mullahs' power, that the mosques are emptying out, is an encouraging sign. Islam will also be changed by the growing disaffection of its faithful. As the philosopher Daryush Shayegan emphasizes, when the Islamic Republic in Teheran collapses, political Islam as a whole will go down with it, including the Sunni world. If the great Persian civilization rejects theocratic hypocrisy and nonsense, the world will breathe more easily.

16

Resistance or Penitence

A good victory makes the vanquished rejoice, and
must have about it something divine which spares
humiliation.

Nietzsche[1]

Listen to the jihadists express themselves while they
are engaging in decapitation and slaughter: they are
sententious barbarians, swaggering executioners proud
to be making an example of their victims by liquidating them as they look into the camera. They quote
scripture, say what is licit and illicit, speaking with a
half-theological, half-juridical passion. Their discourse
oscillates between pedantry and sobbing. These people
are suffering, they have to kill, right now, to relieve their
pain. It is out of the intoxication of self-victimization
that so many young people pass from moderation to
fanaticism. This is a shift that reminds us of the shift
from the far right to Nazism or from Marxism to
Stalinism, which are effected by constituting oneself
as a martyr seeking punishment. We have known this
since at least Dostoevsky and Camus: the aspiration to

absolute freedom can lead to a cult of death and crime. A terrible lesson for the anti-authoritarian generation: forty years after May 1968 and its infantile slogans – 'neither God nor master', 'Live without wasting time and get all the bliss you can' – a fringe of young people, raised in the context of a rejection of paternal or parental authority, prostrates itself in front of little bearded bosses who enslave women and require others to sacrifice their lives. The motto 'I do what I please' leads to voluntary and desired servitude. Someday it will be necessary to rewrite the history of 1968-style hedonism in light of current events: its naive cult of the present moment, its demand for everything *right now*, so well adapted to consumer society, its rejection of procreation and its indifference to the future plunged Europe into a demographic deficit and doubt. The culture of enjoyment went hand in hand with the emphasis on repentance and the weakening of immune-system defences.

Islam is part of the French and European landscape, it is the Old World's second-largest religion, it has the right to be free to worship in its own way, the right to official recognition, to protection by the public authorities, to decent places to pray, and to decent celebrations. On the condition that it respect republican and secular rules, cease being ambiguous about the fundamentalists, and not demand an exceptional status because of its uniqueness. In this domain, as we have said, it must enjoy the same prerogatives and be subject to the same duties as any other religion, no more and no less. Its believers must be protected, of course, but non-believers, liberals, must also be protected. As I argued several years ago,[2] we should create a vast system of aid for dissidents from this religion, encourage divergent voices, offer them financial, moral, or political support, sponsor them, invite them, protect them. Today there is no cause that is graver or more sacred, or that more involves future generations' concord. For too long, with a suicidal recklessness, our continent has bowed down before the religious fanatics and decided to gag or ignore the free thinkers: consider the fact that Tariq Ramadan was for a time an adviser to Tony Blair, and that Great Britain remains open, in the name of freedom of speech, to all the jihad's crusaders. *Blessed be the tepid and the sceptical who cool the ardent river of faith.*

What we need to legislate is the abolition of the crime of apostasy. Everyone must have the right to leave a religion, to freely examine its doctrine, to renew its exegesis, and imams and theologians must be allowed to reinterpret the sacred text as Christians and Jews did in earlier centuries. The panicky desire to spare Islam the test of being challenged is dangerous – especially in the Anglo-Saxon world hemmed in by devotion and political correctness – the way some orientalists want to preserve it as a treasure, no matter what the cost, while condemning a few lateral deviations. The religious persecution of Muslims is obviously unacceptable and must be denounced. But the same protection must be afforded Christians, Jews, Buddhists, Hindus, and Baha'is in Muslim countries. To fail to defend these values everywhere would be to ensure the end of the universalist hope. That is why we must involve our Muslim compatriots in the political, parliamentary, and cultural life of our countries, make them citizens like all others, which most of them already are. In this respect, the election of Sadiq Kahn – a lawyer, a practising Muslim, and the son of Pakistani immigrants (his father was a bus driver) – as mayor of London in May 2016 was welcome news, because it rewarded merit and not membership in a religion. This election cut the ground from under the feet of all those who see Europe as a continent infected by hatred for the Quranic religion.[3]

So what should we do? Draw a distinction between what is our concern and what is not. It is not for us to reform Islam in all its multiplicity, outside our borders; it will become what Muslims want to make of it (André Laurens), especially since the Sunni world, without clergy but not without orthodoxy, is as fragmented as the Protestant world, whereas Shiism, which is pyramidal and hierarchical, is more like the Catholic world (even if the analogy is misleading). What is our concern, at least in part, is the fate of Islam within our borders. Although reforming it is not our job, it is our duty to offer aid to the reformers here in Europe. The challenge, then, is to transform Muslims in France into French Muslims, through a foundation, a charter, or even a concordat, with clear rules, so that citizenship and belonging to the nation take priority over religious convictions. Let's not force Muslims, in France or elsewhere, to make the appalling choice between renunciation and resentment, between collaboration and radicalization. Let's call for a pacified religion, like that practised by most Muslims in our world. For a frank and generous dialogue to take place, we have to put everything on the table, outline concrete proposals as well as draw lines in the sand.[4] Numerous compromises are conceivable (for example, the creation of institutes of Islamic theology and of training for imams), but there are also many impossible concessions (the establishment of a separate law derived from Sharia, for example). Although the state must protect religious diversity, it must also ensure the peaceful coexistence of creeds, including those of sceptics and atheists, since atheism is also a spiritual option.

As for foreign policy, the intelligent thing to do is first to defeat our enemies, immediately, and to support the least extremist groups everywhere. At the same time, we must suggest to the parties concerned that their interest is not to eliminate their adversaries but to live together with each other in tolerance, as Catholics and Protestants learned to do after three centuries of war and ruthless massacres (except for the deplorable example of Northern Ireland, where a religious conflict was accompanied by a colonial conflict). Perhaps with regard to the Islamic bloc it will be necessary to adopt, by constituting a triumvirate consisting of Europe, the United States, and Russia, the policy of containment advocated by George F. Kennan in 1948 with regard to the Soviet bloc: establish a *cordon sanitaire* around nations likely to export violence (Pakistan, Afghanistan, Iran, Iraq, Sunni Syria, Saudi Arabia, Qatar, Sudan, Somalia, Erdoğan's Turkey, etc.), and engage in trade and dialogue with them, but not without reservations.

Europe is entitled to offer itself as a model to an Islamic world prey to chaos and tumult. 'The noble Quran', said Hassan al-Banna, 'designates Muslims as the guardians of humanity and accords them the right of sovereignty and dominion in order to accomplish this sublime mission.'[5] But how can they be the guardians of humanity when they cannot guard themselves, instead providing everywhere an example of arbitrariness, mass cruelty, and division? Sadistic filmed violence and crimes against humanity are always an admission of impotence. Fanaticism is the recourse of the weak: only moderation is a proof of strength. Each time God is placed on the side of murder, courage is placed on the side of non-belief.

In this respect we cannot wish French Muslims to experience what Christians experienced over the course of history, in France at the time of the Revolution and up until 1905, in Spain in the 1930s, or in Mexico starting in 1926, when the government, having decided to de-Catholicize the country, provoked a civil war between *christeros* (soldiers of Christ) and the federal forces. In France, starting in 1791, churches were sacked or burned, prelates hanged or decapitated, priests shot, nuns raped, ecclesiastics drowned *en masse* along with women and children. During the wars in the Vendée (1793–9), Church property was confiscated, and even at the beginning of the twentieth century, convents were surrounded by mobs, nuns were expelled *manu militari*, and congregations were dissolved 'to win the war in the schools'.[6] Integration into democracy can take place with more consideration.

We do not have the right to be stupid in the battle against fanaticism, at the risk of feeding the fire we're trying to put out. Practising blind vengeance, making gratuitous insults, and organizing pogroms plays into the enemy's hands. They want to draw us into an endless cycle of reprisals. To this brutal fury we must oppose an intelligent anger. To all those who have had the good fortune to be by birth or by naturalization American, Canadian, French, German, Swedish, or Dutch, and who have preferred terrorism to involvement in politics, we must reply: too bad for you. You had an extra-ordinary opportunity and you blew it! The problem is not to repeat *urbi et orbi* that Islam is compatible with a republic; it is for Islam to prove it, and for us to help it do so, because if we don't we will all sink into violence. The success of this enterprise is the great challenge of our generation, knowing that Islam is not only a religion, in the strict sense of the term, but also a way of life, an allegiance and the foundation of a collective identity. It is symptomatic that at the time of the 'Arab Spring', mosques were never burned, minarets were not destroyed, and imams or ulama were not hanged the way priests were hanged or churches destroyed every time there was a mass uprising in the West, right down to the twentieth century. That forbids us to project our Western logic onto this great religion.

To make the point in two steps: those who do not like blacks, Arabs, Indians, Asians, Jews, Christians, Muslims, Buddhists, atheists, homosexuals, or free women, those who are hostile to the plurality of ways of life, to the mixing of the great metropolises, to the extraordinary freedom of modern people, should not live in France, in Europe, or, still less, in North America. They should not live in New York, London, Amsterdam, Madrid, Rome, or Copenhagen. They have chosen the wrong century, to borrow a famous expression of Trotsky's. The monochrome, mainly white and Christian Europe and United States are over.

But those who would like to erase the history and personality of European countries, to impose a foreign law on them, to ask them to collaborate in their own decomposition[7] or to transform the natives into interior exiles, have also chosen the wrong century. They must not be surprised by the violent reactions they will arouse, which will resemble the uprisings of nations that were earlier colonized by France, Britain, or Spain. Europe cannot resolve to repudiate itself. Let us recall that the mayor of Rome agreed to veil the statues in the Capitoline Museum during the visit of the Iranian president Rohani in January 2016, and that wine was banned from the protocol long enough for a dinner with the president of Italy, Sergio Mattarella, and the prime minister, Matteo Renzi. Rare has the spirit of capitulation been pushed further. The devil is indeed in the details. If wanting to be oneself has become a crime liable to the worst punishments, then it is likely that a majority of Europeans will be prepared to risk that sanction to persevere in their being. The time has come to choose between Resistance and Penitence.

17

Western Values are
Not Negotiable

We are doubtless deluding ourselves with a dream when
we think that equality and fraternity will someday
reign among human beings without compromising
their diversity. Humanity, however, if not resigned
to becoming the sterile consumer of the values that it
managed to create in the past, is capable only of giving
birth to bastard works, to gross and puerile inven-
tions, and must learn once again that all true creation
implies a certain deafness to the appeal of other values,
even going so far as to reject them if not denying them
altogether. For one cannot fully enjoy the other, identify
with him, and yet at the same time remain different.

Claude Lévi-Strauss[1]

Drinking wine and embracing beauty is better than
sanctimonious hypocrisy.

Omar Khayyam (1048–1131), *The Rubaiyat*

Freedom of expression would not be so important
to us if it were not first a wound: the allergy to the
multitude of our fellows' behaviours and convictions.
The fact that people worship other gods, or worship

none, is *a priori* intolerable. The famous statement attributed to Voltaire – 'I do not agree with what you say but I will fight to the death for your right to say it' – is as noble as it is hollow. The first reflex is always to hold one's ground and maintain that other people's religion and habits are false and scandalous. Their objections are first of all affronts. To surmount this suffering and accept the diversity of beliefs and choices as the norm of an open society, a long education in pluralism is required. A month after the demonstration on 11 January 2015 in memory of the victims at *Charlie Hebdo*, a Catholic philosopher, Fabrice Hadjadj, asked: 'Freedom of expression? Fine! But what do we have to express that is so important?'[2] He had a point, but who determines the importance or the futility of what is expressed? Free expression presupposes many words, vain and empty, which also make possible the appearance of a true expression. Without this humus, without this welter of words, a strong thought could not emerge. As a system, democracy is unique in that it does not kill its adversaries any more than it imprisons them: it admits the conflict of interests, the rotation of power, the legitimacy of discord. We agree to disagree and to settle our differences in an institutional way through elections and courts of law. Britain has even turned opposition to the government into a duty.

We can understand the confusion of a Muslim, a Jew, or a pious Christian in an environment that is not their own, their indignation on seeing posters and images that seem indecent, clothes that anger them. Tempted by 'sin', the righter of wrongs often begins by yielding to it, to fornication, alcohol, or drugs, and redeems himself by killing. For example, according to his father, the killer in Orlando, Florida, Omar Mateen, who murdered forty-nine people in a gay concert hall in June 2016, had decided to act after seeing two men kissing each other on the mouth. He himself had obvious homosexual inclinations. Freedom is a kind of giddiness to which one cannot yield without resistance or remorse. In this sense, jihadism is a crisis of truth. For someone who thinks he is the sole depository of the Truth, all these ways of behaving are an insult to God or to tradition.

One may consider the Western way of life absurd, contrary to decency, and criticize it, turning away from it as a sin – and in fact that is the meaning of the Arabic expression *boko haram* ('Western education is a sin'), from which one of most violent Islamist sects in northern Nigeria takes its name. As it exists, however, despite its imperfections, the modern Western way of life seems preferable to what was done earlier. We are not going to relegate women to the home, cover their heads, lengthen their skirts, get rid of shorts and tight trousers, imprison or re-educate homosexuals, forbid alcohol in public, ban religious caricatures, censor the cinema, the theatre, or literature, codify or limit tolerance in order to avoid offending the finicky sensitivities of a few religious bigots.[3] Let us be wary of the connivance among the three monotheisms, which are prepared to work together to erode our conquests. We are not going to go backwards on the road of History to please the obscurantists of the Crescent or the Cross and their 'progressive' allies. There comes a time when we simply have to say: this is the way we live. Take it or leave it. In Rome, do as the Romans do. And if there is a play, a film, or a cartoon that hurts the feelings of a group or a minority, they can always resort to public protests or to the courts (as Christian conservatives do in France). It is better to file a complaint, shout, or demand damages than to stab or shoot the apostate or the infidel, even though there is a 'juridical jihad' that indirectly designates targets for the killers to attack. If God is truly merciful and omnipotent, it's hard to see how a mortal's graffiti, a woman's free-flowing hair, or a literary hack's scribblings could offend him in any way.

Every time a terrorist attack casts France into mourning, we hear the same litany: we are paying the price for our presumptuous demand that Muslims confine their practices to the private sphere.[4] By a discreet form of blackmail, the authorized voices tell us that our 'secular fundamentalism' (Farhad Khosrokhavar) stigmatizes a whole community, pushing the most talented of the practising Muslims to leave France and the others to embrace the sirens of radical Islam as a 'backup solution'.[5] We are supposed to renounce what we are in order to allow believers to become what they want to be. Or else, as the sociologist Raphaël Liogier says, we are atoning for our obsession with the veil and Islamic fashion at the risk of helping to stage a war between civilizations. Going further, a libertarian neo-conservative explains that 'Islamo-nihilism is a consequence of French intolerance, even if that's not all it is.'[6]

Unfortunately for our analysts, the jihadists strike everywhere, not only in the United States and Germany, but also in Algeria, Tunisia, Egypt, Syria, Iraq, Pakistan, and Nigeria, and these countries do not forbid the veil; in fact they strongly recommend it on pain of the worst punishment. France, we are told, should therefore abandon what constitutes its identify in order to live in peace. Give up your principles, they say, leave that terrible secularity behind, obey the ukases of a minority, and you will experience a few years of respite. Until the next round of demands. Which will not fail to be made, because it is the very existence of France that is the problem.

Can the offence against God be cleansed? Montesquieu's subtle reply: 'The ill came from the idea that the divinity must be avenged. But one must make divinity honoured, and one must never avenge it. Indeed, if one were guided by the latter idea, where would punishments end? If men's laws are to avenge an infinite being, they will be ruled by his infinity and not by the weakness, ignorance, and caprice of human nature.'[7] To apply absolute criteria to imperfect human actions is to take the world into immoderation or madness. It requires great talent to insult God, and overweening pride to believe that we have wounded him or to claim that we are going to cleanse the stain with the blasphemer's blood. Whether one worships or curses him, he remains, assuming that he exists, outside our reach. Evil, Benedict XVI repeated in 2011 from an entirely different point of view, 'is [...] the presumption of acting by oneself, of competing with God and substituting oneself for Him, of deciding what is good and what is evil, of being the master of life and death'.[8] The convenient thing about God (as about Nature) is that he can be made to say anything we want: he will not intervene to contradict us. Anyone who speaks in the name of the All-Powerful is monopolizing a place that belongs to no one. If you want to know what is worst in Western culture – arrogance, vulgarity, violence wrapped in the flag of idealism, lubricious Puritanism – go to North America. It is too bad that Europe often adopts the bad features of the United States while ignoring what it has that is admirable: self-confidence and the ability to restart History on new foundations in every generation. The Old World repeats over and over, the New World begins over and over. The United States: the greatest power of repulsion combined with the greatest power of seduction. We Europeans are obviously cowardly and decadent, torn between our vague desire for total independence and our nostalgia for the past. We are too intelligent to believe in God, but too weak to believe in ourselves, and we repeat, perplexed, this saying of Robespierre's: 'Atheism is aristocratic.' At least we have constructed a civilization that is unique in History, envied by many, founded on prosperity and peace, and combining respect for individuals and the variety of their aspirations. In this respect the hatred of the West is always hatred of law and liberty, and despots the world over know that, from Vladimir Putin to Ali Khamenei, from Raúl Castro to Tayyip Erdoğan. To welcome the West and democracy is to open the door to protesting abuses disguised as eternal laws, as inequalities based on nature. It imposes on all societies insurmountable tasks: freeing themselves from tradition, emerging from the reassuring cocoon of custom in order to invent new ways of being. The West is hated not for its real faults and crimes but for its attempt to correct them. It was one of the first societies to liberate itself from its savagery; it freed itself from monarchical and religious absolutism, inviting the rest of the world to follow it, to enter into crisis in its turn. That is what others cannot pardon it for, beyond its historical and real sins – colonialism, slavery, and imperialism, the curse of which is laid on the West alone, whereas other cultures (the Ottoman Empire, the Arab conquest in Spain, North Africa, and Asia) committed the same sins, but have not yet atoned for them. The true driving force behind fundamentalism is not scrupulous respect for the Scriptures, but the fear of freedom: jihadist leaders often have diplomas,[9] but what motivates them above all is the terror of a way of life based on individual autonomy, perpetual innovation, challenges to authority, and the right to reject accepted truths. The progress of freedom in the world goes hand in hand with hatred of freedoms, and especially of the emancipation of women, a fundamental symbolic mutation.

   Therefore the goal should not be to Islamize Europe, but to Europeanize Islam, to make of it one religion among others that would eventually influence, regarding tolerance, the rest of the *ummah*. The Old World could become the seat of a new criticism and hermeneutics for the Prophet's religion. Islam is plural, but the Islam that is dominant today is a 'thanatocracy', a culture of death (Bruno Étienne). To realize that long-term goal, we have to begin by not capitulating, not renouncing the heart of our heritage: the spirit of examination, the equality of the sexes, religious discretion, respect for individual rights and liberties, freedom of expression. These principles, which have been achieved by the two great revolutions, the American and the French, are not negotiable. But they are accessible to everyone, independently of religious belief, culture, or skin colour.

It is on the strength of these convictions that we can resist terror, the potential death that lurks everywhere, in our cities, streets, railway stations, shopping centres, places of worship, churches, temples, synagogues, mosques. The only way to respond to the emissaries of the Islamist green plague, who are the heirs of the Nazi brown plague of yesteryear, is calmly and with contempt. Like the British at the time of the Blitzkrieg, who resisted, imperturbable and dignified, the German bombardments. Like the Parisians who after the attack at the Bataclan on 13 November 2015 re-occupied the cafés, the theatres and concert halls, and nearby bars. The same thing happened at a café in Tel Aviv, the Max Brenner, which was hit in June 2016 by an attack that killed four people and wounded seven, and which opened the following day as if nothing had happened. Magnificent heroism interwoven with insouciance. Life goes on, stronger than anything. Barbarity kills but does not break.

18

Weary of God

I beg God to relieve me of God.
  Meister Eckhart, a German mystic (1260–1328)

Mosques are our barracks, minarets our bayonets, and
believers our soldiers.
                              Recep Tayyip Erdoğan, 1999[1]

Every time I go into a bookstore, well stocked with
more books than any single person could ever read,
every time I visit a museum or a crowded exhibition,
every time I go to a theatre or cinema in front of which
people are standing in long lines, every time I listen to
an opera, or a classical or jazz concert, I am reminded of
a commonplace that has been repeated *ad nauseam* ever
since the Romantic period and is constantly peddled
by conservatives and fundamentalists of every stripe:
Europe and America live in 'desolation' (Heidegger), a
'spiritual void', a 'desert of values [that] leads people
to resort to daggers' (Régis Debray).[2] 'What had never
been seen, up to now, is civilization built entirely
on something negative, on what might be called an

absence of principles; that is precisely what gives the modern world its abnormal character, what makes it a kind of monstrosity' – so wrote the esoteric author René Guénon in 1927; drawn to the Orient, he ended up converting to Islam, and died in 1951 in Cairo, calling on Allah.[3] Consumerism and capitalism are supposed to have emptied our lives of all meaning and reduced life to the mechanical gestures of producing and purchasing. We are supposed to have become soulless hamsters turning in our treadmill wheels from birth to death, seeking desperately for meaning in our lives. 'Islam can only win, because modernity is incapable of quenching man's thirst for spirituality', said Sayyid Qutb. Behind this refrain, we have to hear a condemnation and a regret: the modern world is bad because we have forgotten God, thereby ceasing to found social law on divine transcendence alone. The end of this sublime ideal is said to have thrown us into platitude and mediocrity, the counterpart of our mad audacity. Deprived of the anchor of the All-High, European societies since 1789 are supposed to have moved toward a generalized collapse, in accord with a mantra reproduced by the Romantics, socialists, anti-moderns, and various families of peevish contemporaries. People repeat the vague prophecies attributed to André Malraux regarding the twenty-first century, which is supposed to be spiritual or not exist at all, without seeing that this spirituality has for the moment taken the ugly form of fanaticism.

If you take away God, the human heart has to be filled with another idol: money, wealth, success. We recall Chateaubriand's dictum: 'if Christianity is destroyed, it will be replaced by Islam'; quote Cioran's quip: 'In fifty years, Notre Dame de Paris will be a mosque'; and expand at length on the theory of communicating vessels, according to which if one vessel is empty, it will be filled by other vessels connected with it. Even

Emmanuel Carrère, praising Michel Houellebecq's novel *Submission*, wrote in a much-noticed article in *Le Monde* (6 January 2015): 'Many well-disposed thinkers once again see this [European] civilization as in danger, and I think this danger is real, but it is not impossible that it might also be fruitful, that Islam might be, in the longer or shorter term, not a disaster, but the future of Europe, just as Judeo-Christianity was the future of the civilization of Antiquity.' Why not? But this need for transcendence that is supposed to relieve us of the problem of existence is above all a need for rituals, for immediate answers. What our period wants is not the elevation of a new religion that will enchant us, but chiefly the simplicity of a creed that avoids insoluble problems. The radical Islam that is spreading today is not the great and marvellous civilization of the Umayyads, the Ottomans, or the Moghuls, it is an ossified and degraded faith eager for revenge and drawing its revival from rivers of blood. Jihadism is not proof of the Muslim religion's spiritual vitality, it is the hideous power of resentment transformed into a machine for killing and massacring. Muhammad – and this is the ambiguity of his message – was not only a prophet but also a warlord, who was often ruthless. Lessons of clemency as well as of violence can be found in the Quran, and this ambivalence is reflected by the literalist commentators, who have a hard time choosing between indulgence and annihilation. Christianity became violent in spite of the Gospels when it became a state religion under Constantine and especially under Theodosius in 380, betraying Christ's message of peace and love. Muslim fundamentalists are faithful to the period of Muhammad's life when he was in Medina (622–32), ferocious and pitiless with regard to infidels and animists, which abolished the open and tolerant earlier period in Mecca.

As for the restoration of the old order desired by the conservatives, it is not a return to the great mystics of the Christian era, St John Chrysostom, St John of the Cross, St Theresa of Ávila, St Benedict, or St Francis of Assisi, and still less to St Augustine or St Thomas. Neither is it the study of the great spiritual or Sufi traditions, of the mystics or Gnostics of the Muslim era, Roumi, al-Ghazali, Ibn Arabi, Mansur Al Allaj, Avicenna, Ibn Khaldoun, Rabia of Basra (an eighth-century woman poet), Abu Nuwas, or Abu Al-Ma'arri (a blind Syrian ascetic and sceptic of the tenth century whose busts were all decapitated by the jihadists of the Al-Nusra Front during the Syrian civil war).[4] It is a simple return to religion as a factor of civil order and pacification, such as it existed before the French Revolution. People would like to return to the ordinary man's faith, to the immediate certainties that we attribute to the naive ways of Old Regime Europe. Apart from the fact that this simplicity is in many respects a retrospective illusion, this spiritual renaissance looks a lot like a regression. It is attractive in so far as it would plunge us into a life laid out in advance and relieve us of the obligation of choosing how to live our lives. Freedom is unbearable because it is the correlate of an ontological insecurity experienced by individuals deprived of the crutches of tradition, religion, and the community. The current trend is not that of a religious revival but that of a thirst for assurance, a demand for ready-made meaning; a demand that life be framed in strict, detailed prescriptions covering all the acts of everyday life (which is what Sharia is).

The moderns' contradiction is they want the freedom to think for themselves and at the same time the viaticum of a catechism that delivers them from that freedom by imposing commandments on them. The maniacal observance of rites – the five prayers, the fasting – does not always attest to a genuine spiritual involvement. Often, it has to do with the uterine warmth of the community, with a mass conformism, not with mystical depth. The return of God that people have been crowing about for twenty years is no more than a show staged for others, not a deepening of faith. Personally, I see few places where intellectual, literary, philosophical, and spiritual life is today richer or more profuse in astonishing works than in old Europe and North America. And this richness proceeds precisely from the uncertainty in which we find ourselves, whether believers or non-believers, with regard to the ultimate questions – whatever the true perils may be, regarding young people and the civilization of the screen, entertainment, and schools that have too often given up on transmitting values.

The Western world is described as a besieged fortress, prey to an implacable adversary. This proposition can be inverted with just as much pertinence: Islam is also under siege as much as it is on the offensive. The West may be in danger of collapsing, but this danger is even greater for Islam. Western societies believe they are helpless, but grossly underestimate themselves. We are stronger than we think. The fanatics are weaker than they think because we have already subverted them from within. We occupy their brains, we haunt their souls, and that is what enrages them. Let us not minimize the extraordinary power of attraction that the Western way of life exercises on foreign peoples, which is the counterpart of their aversion to it. Like us, they are infected by impatience for freedom, the requirement of law, a way of life that combines love of life with the pursuit of happiness and individual achievement. Their dreams are ours.

It is a process that moves in both directions: Enlightenment scintillates as much as it is obscured. What these peoples want to be liberated from is not so much religion as clericalism, bigotry, superstition, foolishness. Rather than mechanically repeat that we are experiencing the return of religiousness, let's ask instead whether we are not living through a worldwide crisis of the great religions (Marcel Gauchet) that explains the current convulsions and lunacy. Part of the Muslim world is being radicalized, not because it is moving away from us in order to return to the age of the caliphate, but because it is moving toward the West and feels threatened, less by scientific innovations than by the freedoms granted. We err in constantly referring to 'the fear of the Other', forgetting that this Other is troubling because he resembles us. It is when people compare themselves with others that they take refuge in sectarian behaviours, in what Freud called 'the narcissism of small differences'. It is proximity that frightens people, not alterity, because the former is accompanied by the possibility that difference will be erased. We fiercely differentiate ourselves by clothing and ostentatious piety for fear of being absorbed by the Other.

It is in fact the dislocation of the old order that we are witnessing everywhere in the East and in Africa. More than a 'clash of civilizations', it is a violent convergence of civilizations. The fundamentalists think they are invading us, beginning a third conquest after the failure of the first two; but they are being conquered in turn, transformed in spite of themselves by their contact with us, and that contamination scares them. In this respect, jihadism, familiar with the latest murderous technologies and cinematic montages worthy of Hollywood's goriest films, betrays a pathology of imitation rather than alterity. It already proceeds from the post-religious. The quest for a lost purity of religion may be, as Nietzsche perceived, a symptom of scepticism and despair.

In addition to its classic divisions, the Arab Muslim world is traversed by a major fault line: a panicky rigid-ification of dogma on the one hand, and an immense weariness with God on the other. God is constantly invoked, governing every detail of everyday life from rising in the morning to going to bed in the evening, directing even people's thoughts, intervening in their ways of washing, of making their ablutions, putting societies under an implacable supervision. Many faithful Muslims would like the opportunity, allowed by other religions, to believe at their own rhythm and in their own way, and especially not to believe, to leave the All-Powerful in the form of a question or a maybe, to be part-time believers. The genius of Christianity in its maturity is to have been able to provide a space for sceptics and agnostics, to permit them to breathe, far from the Holy Scriptures, in order to enter into dialogue with them. *Mocking God is the oxygen of the old monotheisms.* There is nothing sweeter than a great religion in decline, when it renounces violence and prose-lytizing, and emanates nothing but its spiritual message, tinged with an indulgent suspicion. This indulgence is in itself a conquest of wisdom. It is tragic that radical Islam is depriving itself of this dimension, preferring bigotry to doubt, murder to mercy. In this sense, France offers its Muslim citizens who are weary of prayers, incantations, and restrictive rituals a unique oppor-tunity to be relieved of the celestial burden. But God himself is no doubt weary of being constantly invoked by humans who scorn his message, compromising it with all-too-human passions, abusively adorning themselves with his majesty. The American writer Saul Bellow, commenting on the famous German expression *Glücklich wie Gott in Frankreich*' ('happy like God in France'), explained: 'God would be perfectly happy in France because he would not be troubled by prayers, observances, blessings and demands for the interpre-tation of difficult dietary questions. Surrounded by unbelievers He too could relax toward evening, just as thousands of Parisians do at their favourite cafés. There are few things more pleasant, more civilized than a tranquil terrace at dusk.'⁵ What Paris, 'the holy city of secularism', and France in general offer foreigners and the French themselves is the possibility of living well in the silence or discretion of the Divine. This asylum of peace that France shares with few other regions of the world is too precious to be trampled underfoot by a few fanatics. What France asks of its people, no matter what their religious denomination, is that they refrain from practising their religion ostentatiously.[6] The exuberant visibility of the female body is better than the aggressive visibility of the bigots.

God, if he exists, leaves humans the option of conducting their lives as they wish. Religion is not dead, far from it, but it has to maintain in our lives the place of the enigma, not the dogma. 'Why is there something rather than nothing?' Leibniz asked. There are questions whose very nature is to be suspended and not to imply any answer.

19

The Grandeur and the Tragedy of Tolerance

In France, men have much more respect for the female sex; the greatest lords do incredible honours to women of the lowest estate, so that women do what they want and go wherever they please.

Mehmed Çelebi XXVIII[1]

Considering that the Christian religion preceded the Muslim religion in the world by several centuries, I cannot help hoping that Muslim society will one day break its bonds and walk resolutely on the path of civilization, as has Western society, to which the Christian faith, despite its rigors and its intolerance, has not been an invincible obstacle. No, I cannot accept that this hope be taken away from Islam. Here I plead with M. Renan, not the cause of the Muslim religion, but that of several hundred million people who would thus be doomed to live in barbarism and ignorance.

Sayyid Jamal Al-Din Al-Afghani, reply to Ernest Renan, in *Journal de débats*, 1883[2]

In most international airports one finds, behind the restaurants and duty-free shops, a Catholic oratory, a

Protestant chapel, a Muslim prayer hall, a synagogue, and a Buddhist pagoda. This is an exemplary situation: a spatial distribution that is intended merely to be fair – allowing the faithful of every denomination to go there to meditate and possibly to commend their souls to God before risking the flight – reveals to the traveller an upheaval. Simply by being put on the same level, the great religions, and especially the three monotheisms, are simultaneously honoured and devalued: cohabiting in multiplicity, they form so many absolutes relativized by their juxtaposition. The space of comparison is also the space of depreciation. For the past century, the great religions have mourned their lost grandeur. Each is now one religion among others. The Catholic Church's *aggiornamento* at the Second Vatican Council (1962–5) was inspired by the same feeling. Starting with Blaise Pascal's attempt to use the language of non-belief to prove God's existence, and from his famous 'wager', down to Kierkegaard making doubt the driving force behind Christian faith, numerous believers, seeking to defend religion against criticisms based on reason, have involuntarily exposed themselves to the reign of suspicion. Ecumenism and tolerance did not become the Church's official doctrine until more than a hundred years after Kierkegaard's death, even though it is true that Christianity is based on the death of God, crucified like a slave. An astonishing reversal: Rome condemned official anti-Semitism, recognized Judaism as the Church's elder brother, restricted pontifical absolutism, and accepted the validity of other approaches to the divine, those of Protestants, Orthodox Christians, and Muslims, who ceased to be enemies to be vanquished and became partners in the search for the absolute. John Paul II paid homage to Islam for the truths it transmitted regarding Mary, Jesus, and the prophets.[3] Thus the Council abandoned the principle (promulgated by St Cyprian, the bishop of Carthage in the third century) according to which there is no salvation outside the Church, and put all the great religions on the same level of respect. The inter-religious dialogue could thus begin.

What is a Church that admits that other religions also hold the truth, if not a parliament? Rome became one moral authority among others (the party of those who believe in the Gospels in their Vatican version). But is a liberal religion anything other than a deception that is demoralizing for the faithful? Is the wrathful and jealous God of the Bible, the Gospels, or the Quran willing to have competitors? By treating beliefs as equal, tolerance transcends them less than it levels them out and ultimately disarms them. They are reduced to points of view. They have no need to tear down impious sanctuaries because they can live side by side in a neutralized space. How does one put an end to wars of religion? By establishing above them a law that organizes the peaceful coexistence of all of them and infinitely transcends the particular expression of any one of them: 'It does me no injury for my neighbour to say there are twenty gods, or no god', Thomas Jefferson said.

Detaching ecclesiastical power from the state or the ruler, setting strict limits to it, ensuring that worship remains free by confining it to the private domain – that is the wisdom of civilized society. Of course, the coming together of peoples and civilizations is favoured, and worthy meetings where Catholics, Jews, Muslims, and Buddhists are supposed to exchange their respective creeds, listen to their differences, and mutually reassure one another are organized. The discussion groups quickly turn into parallel apologetics in which the rival references to the Absolute collide without meeting: our Muslim brothers are delighted by our understanding of the Quran's *surahs*, but would prefer a genuine conversion. Our Christian brothers respect the

Prophet's message, but nonetheless suggest that the best of Islam is already contained in the Gospels. Our Jewish brothers emphasize, with great deference, everything that the New Testament owes to the Old Testament. As for our Hindu or Buddhist brothers, they are happy to see the attention given them, and to prove their good will by gladly adding our gods and prophets to theirs in their prayers. Everyone is extremely polite but discreetly rejects the slightest proselytism directed at them. That is how discussions among the great religions are transformed into a vast dialogue of the deaf. How could it be otherwise? Although God is one, there are multiple peoples and multiple ways of worshipping him.

That is the tragic uneasiness of the believer: convinced in his heart that he knows the truth, he has to agree to reduce it in public to the status of a personal judgement. Let him pray to whom he wishes, as he wishes, in Latin, Hebrew, Arabic, Pali, Sanskrit, Aramaic, or Mandarin; let him kneel, rock back and forth, prostrate himself, or strike his forehead against the earth, so long as his prayer has no harmful social or political consequences. He experiences his faith as an absolute that is less disavowed or refuted than flattened out, accepted among others. Whether it be under the sign of the Talmud, the Gospels, the Quran, the Gita, or the Five Classics of Confucianism, the believer is forced to take refuge in personal piety or the reassuring enclosure of his community. He will share with other people the same veneration for a God who is master and creator of the Universe, but who does not even have the right to leave the confines of the synagogue, the cathedral, or the mosque (at least in France). And one is not an atheist in Catholicism the way one is an atheist in Islam or Judaism: each religion engenders its own style of disbelief, each has its way of not believing in God.

Born of the horror of religious persecutions, tolerance is first of all the expression of a disabused wisdom:

people can get along with each other only by taking the edge off their convictions in order to enter into the common mould of secular rationality (Max Weber's *Entzauberung*). Tolerance demands that each person file down his certitudes the way we file down the talons and teeth of animals to make them harmless. It therefore begins by setting aside or minimizing what differentiates us and emphasizing what brings us together. Just as parliamentary devices tolerate the expression of divergent passions, it accepts all practices, all rites, on the condition that they are subject to the rule that will draw their fangs. This is the price to be paid for civil peace, and also for freedom of conscience and thus the possibility of scientific and intellectual work: in order to discover 'not everyday truth bound to tradition but a truth that is identically valid for all those who are no longer blinded by tradition',[4] we have to detach individuals from their membership in a group, dry up the source of dogmas and prejudices, and forget myths and fables. We may regret that in the process the most savage impulses and the most refined cultures would both be destroyed in favour of a uniformity that would make humans an impoverished species, the same everywhere. But tolerance cares less about dignity than about security; it produces unity from below, on the basis of the lowest common denominator, and always gives priority to agreement over convictions, even if they are sublime. This is the price of our survival: we absolutely have to contain fervour in order to channel it into less hot-headed movements.

Christianity was humanized in Europe not by internal good will but because the Renaissance, the Reformation, the Enlightenment, and the Revolution not only weakened it as a temporal power but at the same time saved it as a spiritual power. Rome, in parallel with the Protestant churches, had the courage to make amends by undertaking, through the Second

Vatican Council, a vast re-examination of its doctrine, amputating its aggressive aspects, recognizing its errors and its most terrible crimes. It took almost two millennia for Christianity's various denominations to achieve, more or less under duress, a certain kind of temperance. Will we have to wait six centuries for Islam to become gentler, assuming that it follows the path of Christianity, which is absolutely not certain? Periods of ardent faith in the West were also times of abomination, as well as of masterpieces and incontestable progress.

There need be no nostalgia for those periods of 'high spirituality' that presupposed whole categories of the population being put under guardianship. Christianity was redeemed because its teeth were filed down, because it returned to the purity of the Evangelical message, to the pacifism of the first centuries before Theodosius declared it the sole religion of the Empire. It was by moving away from Christ's word that Catholicism became murderous and violent, and it is by returning to the founding text, to literalist piety, that Islam is dangerous. Christianity emerged from violence in its Roman, Byzantine, Orthodox, or Protestant forms only because it emerged from proselytism in its militant and military version. The Roman Church became, despite itself, a parliament, obliged to arbitrate between its diverse factions, from the most liberal to the most fundamentalist. Even if it still sees itself as the sole depository of the true faith, it consents, not without reluctance, to enter into dialogue with atheism, Protestantism, Orthodoxy, Judaism, and Islam. It has practised intolerance out of conviction; now it is forced to be benevolent out of rationality.

In democratic nations, the great religions can no longer imprison or execute for blasphemy or faithlessness those who contradict them. This is a considerable step forward. The abandonment of violent or forced conversion is a genuine advance, and it explains why

Christianity has become synonymous with gentleness (so gentle that it is now persecuted again). The more amiable a great religion becomes, the more it resolves to be indulgent. The hope of seeing Christianity reunified some day is naive because the various Lutheran, Calvinist, Baptist, Episcopalian clergies, along with the diverse autocephalous clergies of the East or of Africa, prosper in their plurality and not in a false unity. Sooner or later, every monotheism ends up becoming a *de facto* polytheism, the approaches to God multiplying as humanity itself diversifies. Thus we have to hope that the Prophet's religion – already split between Shiites and Sunnis, Sufis, Druses, and Ismailians, modernists and rigorists, Salafists and Muslim Brothers, and rival groups plotting mischief – keeps on dividing, that the *Fitna* (discord) between its different branches, schools, groups, sects, and allegiances deepens.[5] It is tempting to say about it what François Mauriac said about Germany in 1949, when the German Federal Republic was created: 'I like it so much that I'd like to have at least two of them.' I like Islam so much that I'd like to have at least ten, at least a hundred of them. Plurality is the future of the great religions.

In all the cities of Europe, Australia, India, or North America, the streets and avenues are lined on both sides by countless churches, temples, synagogues, and pagodas, all neatly lined up as if on parade, suiting everyone in accord with his affinities. Is that a sign of religious devotion? Perhaps. But especially of civil peace, of the tranquil coexistence of diverse expressions of the divine: not a universal reconciliation of religions, but their frictionless cohabitation, each constituting for the others a positive challenge in a competition of religions. 'Where there is only one religion, tyranny reigns; where there are many, freedom occurs' (Voltaire). In other words, it is religion that stops religion: the legitimacy granted to one stops where the legitimacy of the others begins. In this respect the 'missionary revival' among French Catholics seems legitimate. The stronger Christianity is, the better behaved Islam will be. The best thing one can hope for the latter is not 'phobia' or 'philia', but benevolent indifference in a spiritual market open to all beliefs. Kindness out of detachment is better than malevolence out of enthusiasm. But the fundamentalists have no interest in becoming ordinary: that would mean that Islam is one religion among others, not the One and Only that makes the others obsolete. That's the whole problem!

Epilogue

On History as a Warning

Yet where danger lies
Grows that which saves.

Hölderlin

Since 11 September 2001, since New York, Madrid,
London, Paris, Boston, Brussels, and Berlin, the Western
world has left 'the golden age of security' (Stefan
Zweig). The alliance of law, the market, and democracy,
promised by the new prophets after 1989, was shaken
at the same time as the Twin Towers. Europe no longer
loved History: it thought it had emerged from this
nightmare the first time in 1945, and again after the fall
of the Berlin Wall. It protected itself against this poison
by means of norms, rules, and procedures, out of a
pathological allergy to confrontation, delighted to be
sheltered from storms. For a sanitized people numbed
by the twofold cocoon of consumerism and peace, the
attacks marked the return of the fatality that goes for
our throats, forcing us to espouse its course or die in
terror. Terror situates us in the universe of warning, of a
choice between life and death. The brief cycle of respite

that began with the fall of the Wall on 9 November 1989 ended on 11 September 2001, with the fall of the World Trade Center towers. Peace was merely a parenthesis, prosperity has not calmed religious furies, wars are breaking out again, all the more murderous because they are based on not distinguishing between civilians and combatants.

Islam is not only a problem, it is also a symptom. When the bearded men want to express their aversion to the West, they don't have to look far; they have only to dig around in the literature and philosophy of Europe over the last two centuries. We give them the weapons they use to attack us. The prosecution of Europe is pursued briskly and enthusiastically by Europe itself. Proud to be beating its breast so ostentatiously, it claims a universal and apostolic monopoly on barbarity. The Old World has vanquished all its monsters – slavery, colonialism, fascism, Stalinism – except one: self-hatred. Our guilty conscience is not remorse for a specific crime; for many people it has become an identity, the second home of the afflicted, a convenient refuge for withdrawing from the world. The accursed cast-off of the criminal is a comfort justifying our abdication. Against whom are we fighting? First of all, against ourselves, our scruples, our devouring doubts. We should fear less the virulence of the fools of God than the hatred we have for ourselves and that commands us to surrender. It is obvious that a continent that does not love itself cannot be loved by others, and is psychologically preparing itself for death. It can be colonized because it has become mentally colonizable.

But our enemy, in his savagery, is doing us a favour. If he terrorizes us, he also sharpens our understanding of adversity, reawakens our spirit of resistance. In spite of himself, the enemy has restored our flag and patriotism to us. He has restored fervour and flesh to the old European nations. He has made the soldier and the policeman once again positive heroes in the service of their community. Above all, this leads us to distinguish what falls within the domain of military operations and what falls within that of the conflict of ideas. We will not win this war solely with spies, tanks, and planes – at the risk of reproducing the American hyper-power that has lurched from defeat to defeat for the past fifty years. We will win it first of all on the cultural level, if we persuade ourselves and the rest of the world of the eminent virtues of our civilization and our mores. As in the era of fascism and communism, the battlefield involves thought, networks, media, argumentation, and especially a fastidious attention to the meaning of words. Let us not dream about a premature reconciliation. First we have to lance the boil, defeat the adversary before offering him a helping hand. This reawakening of the religious, in its obscurantist form, forces us to reconsider everything that we take for granted: secularism, the equality of men and women, the democratic system, freedom of expression, loving tolerance, the status of faith and impiety. It imposes on modernity the duty of taking stock. What seemed to go without saying has to be rethought in view of the arguments of religious believers and theologians who are determined not to concede anything to our permissive societies. Every crisis is an opportunity to reform ourselves. We will not emerge unharmed from this trial: we will either be broken or, instead, strengthened in our self-confidence and our capacities for action.

Even if there is no doubt that jihadist nihilism will be defeated before the end of this century – but at the price of how many million dead? – let us grant that an enemy has been born to us and is helping us become once again vigilant and proud of what constitutes us. This is a time to say, with Thucydides, 'Your hostility does us less harm than your friendship.' The adversary puts us

in the contradictory position of wanting to overcome
him and wanting to preserve the energy he breathes into
us. One does not choose one's time, and one does not
choose to be of it or not of it. It bursts upon our lives,
without our seeing it coming, and enjoins us to respond
to it or disappear. We are living in a terrible period. But
as appalling as it is, it is also passionate. It is impossible
to escape the challenge of the century now beginning:
in collaboration with the enlightened or moderate
Muslims who are its main victims, we must defeat the
fanaticism of the Islamists. For this immense task, there
will never be too many people of good will.

Notes

Introduction

1   André Quellien, *La Politique musulmane dans l'Afrique occidentale française* (1910), Paris: Hachette Livre BnF, 2013.

2   Maurice Delafosse, *Revue du monde musulman*, vol. XI, no. V, 1910, p. 57. We are indebted to Abdellali Hajjat and Marwan Mohammed for having presented these forgotten texts in their book *Islamophobie. Comment les élites françaises fabriquent 'le problème musulman'*, Paris: La Découverte, 2016, pp. 73–4. See also Isabelle Kersimon and Jean-Christophe Moreau, *Islamophobie. La contreenquête*, Paris: Plein Jour, 2014, Chapter 1, 'Les aventures d'un concept', which seeks to complement and refute the preceding work.

3   See Maxime Rodinson, *La Fascination de l'Islam*, Paris: Maspero, 1980; rpt. Presses Pocket, 1993.

4   Quoted by Jacques de Saint Victor, 'Du blasphème dans la république', *Le Débat* (Gallimard), May–August 2015, p. 12; see also his historical work *Blasphème. Brève histoire d'un 'crime imaginaire'*, Paris: Gallimard, 2016.

Chapter 1

1   François Ascensi, ex-communist delegate, elected in Seine-Saint-Denis, a member of the Front de gauche.

2   Alfred Marie-Jeanne, politician and president of the Martinique independence movement.

3   See Raymond Aron, *The Opium of the Intellectuals* (1955), trans. D. J. Mahoney and B. C. Anderson, London: Routledge, 2001.

4   On 30 September 2016, at St Louis University, a speech on radical Islam given by Allen West, a retired US Army colonel who served in Iraq and Afghanistan, caused about a hundred students close to the Muslim Brotherhood to walk out as a sign of protest. See William Nardi, The College Fix, 30 September 2016, https://www.thecollegefix.com/post/29261.

5   de Saint Victor, 'Blasphème dans la république', p. 15.

6   Claude Lévi-Strauss, *Le Regard éloigné*, Paris: Plon, 1983, pp. 15–16; *The View from Afar*, trans. J. Neugroschel, Chicago: Chicago University Press, 1992, p. xv.

Chapter 2

1   Quoted in Alexandre Devecchio, *Les Nouveaux Enfants du siècle*, Paris: Cerf Éditions, 2016, p. 72, and available on dailymotion.com. Tarek Obrou's views subsequently changed. Made a knight of the Legion of Honour by Alain Juppé and threatened by ISIS, he might become the Grand Mufti of the Republic.

2   On this subject, see the editorials that followed the 2005 terrorist attacks in London, by Jonathan Freedland in the *Guardian* and by the future mayor of London, Boris Johnson, in the *Daily Telegraph*. Cited in 'La Question postcoloniale', *Hérodote*, 2006, pp. 195–6.

3   According to an iFOP-*La Croix* poll conducted in July 2011.

4   'Kamel Daoud recycle les clichés orientalistes les plus éculés', *Le Monde*, 12 February 2016.

5   In the meantime, the imam, a former activist of the Islamic Salvation Front, was sentenced on 8 March 2016 to six months in prison without parole by a court in Oran, Algeria.

6   *Le Monde*, 7 May 2016, quoted by Raphaelle Bacqué and Ariane Chemin.

7   On the Zaman France website.

8   'The figure of the turncoat [...] is represented by the
      Muslim intellectuals called "moderates" (Abdennour
      Bidar, Malek Chebel, Abdelwahab Meddeb, Mohamed
      Sifaoui et al.), feeding the common view of Islam,
      notably on the subject of prohibiting the wearing of
      the *hijab* in French public schools, and justifying the
      visceral Islamophobia of Oriana Fallaci in Italy.' Hajjat
      and Mohammed, *Islamophobie*, p. 117, note B. What
      relation is there between these authors and Oriana
      Fallaci? None, of course, but as in any unfounded
      accusation, hotchpotches are de rigueur.
9   'Neither Whores nor Doormats'. The goal of this feminist
      association, founded in the 1990s by Muslim women
      in the predominantly Muslim immigrant suburbs and
      public housing projects, is to denounce acts of violence
      against women.
10   Hajjat and Mohammed, *Islamophobie*, p. 139, note B,
      regarding Christine Tassin.
11   Pierre Tevanian, *La Haine de la religion*, Paris: La
      Découverte, 2013, p. 108.
12   Houria Bouteldja, *Les Blancs, les Juifs et nous*, Paris: La
      Fabrique Editions, 2016, p. 76.
13   'Comment les élites françaises fabriquent "le problème
      musulman"', Hajjat and Mohammed, *Islamophobie*.
14   Sylvain Gouguenheim, *Aristote au mont SaintMichel.
      Les racines grecques de l'Europe chrétienne*, Paris: Le
      Seuil, 2008. On this polemic, see the commentary by
      Rémi Brague, who urges that a distinction be drawn
      between Islam as a religion and Islam as a civilization,
      and points out that the Quran was known in Europe
      only from the twelfth century on, and commented upon
      for the first time by Nicholas of Cusa in the fifteenth
      century. Islam's contribution and its continuation of
      the Greek heritage are real. But this recognition of
      debts must not be seen as comparable to the pouring
      of a liquid from one vessel to another: we owe Arabs
      mathematics, astronomy, alchemy, and the Toledo trans-
      lation of Aristotle, and on this latter point Avicenna's
      contribution was the most crucial. But Greek literature,
      Plato, and Plotinus passed directly from Constantinople

to Europe in the fifteenth century. In the end, Europe benefited from these sources only because, starting in the eleventh century, it had carried out an enormous self-examination that made its subsequent Renaissance possible. The receiver has to make itself capable of appropriating the knowledge offered (*La Nef*, no. 194, June 2008).

Chapter 3

1 Houellebecq was acquitted by the Paris criminal court on 22 October 2002. On this subject, Claude Lévi-Strauss, in an interview that appeared on 10 October 2002 in the *Nouvel Observateur*, said: 'I said what I think about Islam in *Tristes Tropiques*. Although in more refined language, it wasn't that far from what Houellebecq has now been put on trial for. Such a trial would have been inconceivable half a century ago; it wouldn't have occurred to anyone. We have the right to criticize religion. We have the right to say what we think. We are contaminated by Islamic intolerance. The same goes for the current idea that we have to introduce the teaching of religions in the schools. [...] There again, that seems to me a concession made to Islam, to the idea that religion should enter areas outside its domain. On the contrary, it seems to me that pure, hard-line secularism has worked very well up to now.'

2 Bernard Lewis, *What Went Wrong? Western Impact and Middle Eastern Response*, Oxford: Oxford University Press, 2001, p. 4.

3 Anne Bernas, 'Les Voix du monde', Radio France Internationale, 3 April 2015.

4 Tevanian, *La Haine de la religion*, pp. 65–6.

5 Ibid., p. 67.

6 I pointed this out in *The Tears of the White Man: Compassion as Contempt*, trans. W. Beer, New York: Free Press, 1986, and especially in *The Tyranny of Guilt*, trans. S. Rendall, Princeton: Princeton University Press, 2012.

7 Régis Debray, *Ce que nous voile le voile. La République et le sacré*, Paris: Gallimard, 2004, pp. 30–1.

8   Régis Debray, 'Le curseur des délicatesses est passé du sexe au religieux', *Le Monde*, 21 September 2015.

9   Hamadi Redissi, *Le Pacte de Nadjd: Ou comment l'islam sectaire est devenu l'islam*, Paris: Seuil, 2007.

10   Emmanuel Todd, *Qui est Charlie?*, Paris: Seuil, 2015; *Who is Charlie?*, trans. A. Brown, Cambridge: Polity, 2015. In this book, Todd claims that Muhammad is 'the central character in the religion of a group that is weak and discriminated against', and Islam is a religion of the poor, whereas the 'zombie Catholicism' that prevails in metropolitan France expresses the reaction of a Vichyist and Islamophobic people. To praise Islam, which is his strictest right, Todd has to trample on Christianity.

Chapter 4

1   Bernard Lewis, *Le Retour de l'Islam*, Paris: Gallimard, 1985, p. 444.

2   Claude Lévi-Strauss, *Tristes Tropiques*, trans. J. Weightman, London: Penguin, 1992 [1955], p. 403.

3   Available at https://www.marxists.org/archive/harman/1994/xx/islam.htm.

4   Alain Badiou, *Notre mal vient de plus loin*, Paris: Fayard, 2016; *Our Wound is Not So Recent*, trans. S. Spitzer, Cambridge: Polity, 2016.

5   On the fact that the European left has ceased to have any understanding of religious phenomena, see Jean Birbaum's excellent essay, *Un silence religieux. La gauche face au djihadisme*, Paris: Seuil, 2016. The orientalist Bernard Lewis had already pointed out this blindness in his book, *The Return of Islam*.

6   Abdelwahab Meddeb, *La Maladie de l'islam*, Paris: Seuil, 2005, Chapter 1.

7   Edwy Plenel, *Pour les musulmans*, Paris: La Découverte, 2015.

8   Michel Foucault, *Dits et écrits*, pp. 747–8, quoted in Julien Cavagnis, 'Foucault et le soulèvement iranien', *Cahiers philosophiques*, no. 130, 2012.

9   'Inutile de se soulever?', *Le Monde*, 11–12 May 1979.

10   See Ayatollah Khomeini, *The Little Green Book*, trans. H. Slemson, New York: Bantam, 1985. In this book

Khomeini reasserts the absolute superiority of the Quran over any other form of religion and relegates the Western world to its Satanic origin: 'Europe [the West] is nothing but a collection of unjust dictatorships; all of humanity must strike these troublemakers with an iron hand if it wishes to regain its tranquility' (p. 2). 'If Islamic civilization had governed the West, we would no longer have to put up with these barbaric goings-on unworthy even of wild animals. If the punitive laws of Islam were applied for only one year, all the devastating injustices and immoralities would be uprooted. Misdeeds must be punished by the law of retaliation: cut off a thief's hands; kill the murderer instead of putting him in prison, flog the adulterous woman or man. Your concerns, your "humanitarian" scruples are more childish than reasonable. Under the terms of Qur'anic law, any judge fulfilling the seven requirements (that he have reached puberty, be a believer, know the Qur'anic laws perfectly, be just, and not be affected by amnesia, or be a bastard, or be of the female sex) is qualified to dispense justice in any type of case. He can thus judge and dispose of twenty trials in a single day, whereas Occidental justice might take years to argue them out' (p. 15).

11   Jean Baudrillard, in *Le Monde*, 13 February 1980. On 3 November 2001, again in *Le Monde*, Baudrillard made the same jubilant commentary on the collapse of the Twin Towers in New York.

12   Quoted by Michel Contat in *Le Point*, 18 March 2013. The French delegation included, among others, Leila Abou-Saif, Claire Brière, Catherine Clément, Françoise Gaspard, and Paula Jacques.

Chapter 5

1   Albert Camus, *The Rebel*, trans. A. Bower, New York: Knopf, 1956, p. 234.

2   Rodinson, *La Fascination de l'Islam*, p. 100.

3   Sophie Peeters, 'Femme de la rue, Bruxelles', dailymotion.com, July 2012.

4   She recounted this event in the magazine *Elle* on 6 November 2006.

5   'Anti-colonialists are universalists who have little interest in the past or in the specific characteristics of the present, which they see as vestiges of a barbarian age that must be destroyed. On the other hand, exoticism leads colonial politicians to try to preserve archaisms, to ally themselves with native preservationists, and to denounce nationalist intellectuals, whether they are reformers or revolutionaries, leaning toward socialism or not, as pale imitators of Europe driven by abstract, poorly understood ideas to destroy their own patrimony.' Rodinson, *La Fascination de l'Islam*, pp. 96–7.

6   Pierre Tevanian compares the 2004 law prohibiting the veil and other religious signs in the schools to the ceremony organized in Algiers on 13 May 1958 by Mme Salan, the wife of the commander of the French Armed Forces in Algeria, at which Muslim women were exhibited on a podium burning their veils as a sign of emancipation (*La Haine de la religion*, p. 116). In other words, to ask French citizens to take off their veils in school is to show colonialism.

7   Rokhaya Diallo, *Racisme, mode d'emploi*, Paris: Larousse, 2011, p. 138. Note that the title of this book is above all programmatic: how can one be racist without running afoul of the law?

8   Marianne.net, 12 June 2016.

9   'Musulmans, changeons de logiciel', *Le Monde*, 29 July 2016. Abderrahim Hafidi also asks the Muslims of France to stop praying in the streets and to no longer listen to those who, like Tariq Ramadan, imprison young people 'in an identitarian radar that is desiccating and lethal'.

10   Tareq Obrou, *Le Monde*, 4 October 2013.

11   Hajjat and Mohammed, *Islamophobie*, pp. 247 and 248.

12   Raphael Liogier, *Le Mythe de l'islamisation*, Paris: Seuil, 2012. 'Salafism is an Amish Fundamentalism, a Hypermodern Tendency', *Le Point*, 19 September 2016.

13   Olivier Roy, *En quête de l'Orient perdu*, Interviews with Jean-Louis Schlegel, Paris: Seuil, 2014, pp. 288 and 286. Let us recall that in 2009 Switzerland voted to prohibit

the construction of new minarets, a measure that one might find questionable but which does not oblige the state to destroy the old ones. Olivier Roy's comparison is thus specious and polemical.

14 Olivier Roy, *La Sainte Ignorance*, Paris: Seuil, 2008.
15 Michael Walzer, 'Islamism and the Left', *Dissent*, Winter 2015.

Chapter 6

1 *Dictionnaire philosophique*, Paris: Garnier-Flammarion, 1964, p. 190.
2 Quoted in an article that appeared on the website rue89. nouvelobs on 18 January 2016.
3 *Revue du crieur*, no. 3, Paris: La Découverte, pp. 51f. In February 2016, the engineer Mohamed Louizi suspended his blog on Mediapart because of the indulgence and complicity shown by its director, Edwy Plenel, toward Islamism, the Muslim Brotherhood, and the fundamentalist Tariq Ramadan. According to him, Mediapart had become 'an instrument of frérosalafist anti-secular and anti-republican propaganda'.
4 Rokhaya Diallo, *À nous la France!*, Paris: Michel Lafon, 2012, pp. 47 and 48.
5 Here I refer to my book *The Tears of the White Man*.
6 Regarding the alleged hatred of Islam and the cowardice of *Charlie*'s cartoonists, Caroline Fourest points out that only 4 per cent of the magazine's covers were devoted to Muslims; most of its criticism was reserved for political satire and Christian fundamentalists (*Éloge du blasphème*, Paris: Grasset, 2015, p. 100).
7 Alain Badiou, 'Penser les meurtres de masse', a talk given at the theatre of the commune of Aubervilliers on 23 November 2015.
8 Michel Onfray, 'La France doit cesser sa politique islamophobe', *Le Point*, 19 November 2015.
9 It is legitimate to say that we have to discuss the pertinence of military interventions: although the second Gulf War, based on a lie, was disastrous (except for the Kurds, the Shiites, and 80 per cent of the Iraqi population, which was freed from the control of the Baath party),

other military interventions were necessary. The interventions in Mali in 2012 and in the Central African Republic in 2013, not to mention Operation Barkhane, which has contained jihadism in the Sahel, have proven useful. Here Michel Onfray combines a frenetic anti-Americanism with a deliberate misunderstanding of the geostrategic situation. He pulls fabulous numbers out of his hat; the United States and France are supposed to be responsible for the death of 4 million Muslims (*Le Point*, 28 July 2016), why not 10 million, while he's at it? All that to support his thesis. In a note for the Foundation of Strategic Research (February 2016), Bruno Tertrais points out that Palestinian and Iranian terror attacks struck French soil as early as the 1970s, without French armies having intervened abroad. In 2000, a plan for an attack on the Strasbourg cathedral was foiled, even though at that time France was not involved militarily anywhere. Not striking in Afghanistan in 2001 would have allowed a Taliban emirate to prosper and operate the world over. Germany is also threatened as a Crusader country, although it has few troops outside its borders. ISIS wants to imprison us in an intolerable dilemma: submission or intervention. It is too bad that political officials, such as Dominique Villepin, and intellectuals allow themselves to be caught in this trap. The pretexts invoked by the jihadists are confused with the real causes. France is hated for what it is, not for what it does.

10   Marianne, 1 August 2016.
11   Lepoint.fr, 15 January 2015.
12   For example, see the journalist Edwy Plenel: 'these monsters are the product of our society. It is not Islam that has produced these terrorists. The latter appeal to Islam but have nothing to do with it. On the other hand, they are the product of all the fractures, of all the rents, in our society.' Bondy Blog, 14 January 2015.
13   Suleiman Mourad, *La mosaïque de l'islam*, Paris: Fayard, 2016, pp. 112–13.
14   Roy went to Afghanistan at a time when others were tramping around Kathmandu, as he recounts in his

book of interviews with Jean-Louis Schlegel, *En quête de l'Orient perdu*. Roy is typical of those experts who love their subject so much that nothing is allowed to blemish it. Specializing in Central Asia, in 1992 he published a book entitled *L'Échec de l'islam politique* (The Failure of Political Islam), Paris: Seuil, 1992, but never admitted his mistake. Since then he has become entangled in abstruse justifications, similar to the contortions of old communists defending tooth and nail the proposition that the USSR's record was on the whole positive.

15 Olivier Roy, 'Les religions dans l'arène publique', *Esprit*, February 2016, p. 58.

Chapter 7

1 Bernard Lewis, *The Jews of Islam*, Princeton: Princeton University Press, 1984; new edition, 2014, p. 45. The massacre was supposed to punish Joseph ibn Nagrela, a Jewish vizier who had grown too powerful. According to Lewis, such massacres and diatribes were relatively rare in the Islamic world – in comparison with the Christian world, where they were common coin.

2 Edward Said, *Orientalism*, New York: Vintage, 1979, p. 285.

3 Enzo Traverso, *La Fin de la modernité juive. Histoire d'un tournant conservateur*, Paris: La Découverte, 2013.

4 Yvan Najiels, Mediapart, Le Club, espace de libre expression, 9 February 2014.

5 Matthias Küntzel, *Djihad et haine des Juifs*, Paris: Editions du Toucan, 2015, p. 108, quoting Bernard Lewis, *The Jews in Islam*, Princeton: Princeton University Press, 1987, pp. 25–6.

6 Collectif, *Le Monde*, 22 December 2009, quoted in Mathieu Bock-Cote, *Le Multiculturalisme comme religion politique*, Paris: Cerf Éditions, 2016, p. 145.

7 In his film *Malcolm X*, released in 1992, Spike Lee shows clearly how Malcolm X, revolted by the segregation of blacks in the United States, moved from an attitude of anti-white and anti-Semitic aggressiveness when he belonged to the Nation of Islam to a more open humanism after he made a pilgrimage to Mecca.

That was when his former comrades-in-arms, who were jealous of his aura, had him executed.

8   Quoted in Hajjat and Mohammed, *Islamophobie*, p. 185.
9   Ibid., p. 188.
10   Said, *Orientalism*, p. 361, n. 26.
11   Shlomo Sand, 'From Judeophobia to Islamophobia', *Jewish Quarterly*, vol. 57, no. 1, 2010, p. 194. Here Sand forgets the complexity of European history, for example the alliance between Francis I and Suleiman the Magnificent in 1536 against the House of Habsburg's hints of domination. This 'sacrilegious alliance of the crescent with the fleur-de-lys', which was renewed in 1604, allowed the Ottomans to pursue jihad as far as Vienna in 1683. In 1529 the Holy Roman Emperor, Charles V, planned an alliance with Shiite Persia in order to launch an attack on the Ottoman Empire's rear (Matthieu Guidere, 'Petite histoire du djihadisme', *Le Débat*, August 2015, p. 43). Along the same line of thought, Italy (notably, Milan, Mantua, and Florence) constantly made alliances with the Ottoman Empire in order to attack Venice, while in 1493 Pope Alexander VI received the ambassador of the Grand Turk in Rome to denounce Charles VIII of France's plans for a crusade (Rodinson, *La Fascination de l'Islam*, p. 54).
12   Olivier Roy, 'Le burkini n'a rien de fondamentaliste', *Le Point*, 21 August 2016.
13   Rodinson, *La Fascination de l'Islam*.
14   Ibid., pp. 58, 65, 67, 69, 71, 81.

Chapter 8
1   'La Shoah? le sujet colonial en a connu des dizaines. Des exterminations? A gogo', Bouteldja, *Les Blancs, les Juifs et nous*, p. 111.
2   Setting aside the fact that it is hard to see who would want to perpetrate a genocide against Islam in general, apart from soldiers of al-Qaeda or ISIS seeking purification, Sir Iqbal Sacranie includes among the victims of the 'Arabo-Muslim genocide' the Palestinians and Iraqis but not the Kurds gassed by Saddam Hussein. The only 'good' Arab Muslim victims are the ones killed by

non-Muslims. After the *fatwa* against Salman Rushdie, Sacranie declared that death was still too easy for him, and that his torment for his crime had to last as long as possible. He later denied ever having said this.

3 A militant anti-colonialist and a declared revisionist, Serge Thion, who was close to Pol Pot, has always denied the genocidal nature of the Khmer Rouge regime, just as did the philosopher Alain Badiou. He then moved closer to Robert Faurisson and the far-left publishing house La Vieille Taupe, headed by Pierre Guillaume, and published a book in honour of Faurisson, with a note by Noam Chomsky included, without his permission, as a preface. After 11 September 2001, he joined the Islamist trends and supported Dieudonné and anti-Semitic black supremacist groups.

4 Lewis, *Le Retour de l'Islam*, p. 482.

5 Mourad, *La mosaïque de l'islam*, pp. 33, 35.

6 Quoted in Bernard Lewis, *Juifs en terre d'Islam*, Paris: Flammarion, 1986, p. 50.

7 In his historical work, Bernard Lewis notes that in Morocco, Jews had to leave the ghetto barefoot or wearing straw slippers (*The Jews of Islam*, p. 36). For Ayatollah Khomeini, the infidel – whether Christian, Jew, Hindu, Zoroastrian, or Baha'i – was a source of pollution, like urine, excrement, and rotting flesh. Only a conversion to Islam could purify him (p. 34). In counterpoint, we must also remember the courageous act of the sultan of Morocco, the young Mohammed V, who refused to apply Vichy's decrees to his Jewish subjects in 1940, as much out of conviction as out of a desire to assert his independence from the colonial power. At the time, the sherif's kingdom was a protectorate administered by a Resident.

8 In Tunisia, where there were 105,000 Jews in 1951, there now remain about 1,500, distributed among Djerba, Tunis, Sousse, and Gabès. In Morocco, where there were between 230,000 and 280,000 Jews in 1948, there are supposed to be between 2,500 and 3,000 today, mostly in Casablanca and Rabat, protected by the sherifian monarchy.

9   A few eloquent statistics: at the beginning of the twentieth century, the Eastern Christians represented one quarter of the Middle East's population. Today, with all communities taken together and divided into six main denominations, they are no more than 11 million out of the 320 million inhabitants of the region. Except in Jordan, where the Hashemite dynasty protects them, they are everywhere the object of harassment and pressure, especially in Egypt, where they represent the largest Christian community in the Arab world, almost 6 million. Their gradual eradication is also tragic for good relations between Shiites and Sunnis, because the Christians were part of the region's conjunctive ethnic and denominational fabric, and maintained a space of plurality. But to support the Eastern Christians would be to show a very political compassion, we are told by a left-wing scholar (Camille Lons, *Orient XXI*, 26 April 2016), and would inevitably amount to moving to the extreme right, of course...

Chapter 9

1   Quoted in Lewis, *Les Juifs en terre d'Islam*, p. 56.
2   Enzo Traverso, 'Les Juifs et la ligne de couleur', in *De quelle couleur sont les Blancs?*, ed. Sylvie Laurent and Thierry Leclère, Paris: La Découverte, 2013, pp. 253–61.
3   Ibid., p. 60.
4   Curiously, the Chinese arouse no compassion or interest on the part of anti-racist groups. Similarly, the Ligue des droits de l'homme and SOS Racisme refused to support the march organized by the Chinese community on 4 September 2016 after the death of a Chinese dressmaker in Aubervilliers, on the grounds that the goal of this march was to strengthen security and video-surveillance (*Le Monde*, 5 September 2016).
5   Tevanian, in *De quelle couleur sont les Blancs?*, p. 73.
6   Ibid., p. 28.
7   For example, the 'de-colonial' camp planned for the summer of 2016 by 'anti-racist' militants. Or the 'non-white words' organized at the University of

Paris-VIII in the spring of the same year. The 'Nuit Debout' movement that privatized the Place de la République for a few weeks in the spring of 2016 organized feminist meetings in which 'cisgenres', that is, white heterosexual males, were forbidden to participate. Alain Jakubowicz, president of 'International League against Racism and anti-Semitism' (LICRA), called this an 'inverted Ku Klux Klan' in which the only criterion is skin colour.

8   Tevanian, in *De quelle couleur sont les Blancs?*, p. 28.
9   Ibid., pp. 32, 33.
10 See https://www.marianne.net/debattons/tribunes/lettre-ouverte-au-monde-musulman.
11 Marie Darrieussecq, 'Pour Christiane Taubira', *Le Monde*, 17–18 November 2013.
12 Quoted by Francois Bedarida, 'La mémoire contre l'histoire', *Esprit*, July 1993, p. 9. Cf. Houria Bouteldja, who says the same thing, addressing Jews: 'You are not the true chosen people. You are being lied to' (*Les Blancs, les Juifs et nous*, p. 50).
13 Bouteldja, *Les Blancs, les Juifs et nous*, p. 51. A sign of the times: in his editorial for the month of August 2016, the director of *Le Monde diplomatique*, Serge Halimi, condemned Houria Bouteldja's obsession with race and his indulgence toward Ahmadinejad.
14 Vladimir Jankelevitch, *L'Imprescriptible*, Paris: Seuil, 1996, pp. 19–20.
15 Marion Van Renterghem, 'L'antisémitisme impulsif de cinq gars sans problèmes', *Le Monde*, 20 February 2015.
16 Laurent Mucchielli, 'Le retour de l'antisémitisme', the ritual speech given at CRIF's annual dinner. In the same speech, Mucchielli sees the development of Islamophobia in French public opinion as more important than the already well-documented anti-Semitism.
17 Ilan Halimi was kidnapped, tortured, and killed in 2006 by the 'les Barbares' gang, on the grounds that, being a Jew, he must be rich. In 2012, Mohammed Merah killed in cold blood three young children and a teacher at the Ozar Hatorah school in Toulouse. For some people these

'exploits' made him a hero. In January 2015, during the attack on the Hyper Cacher supermarket at the Porte de Vincennes, Amedy Coulibaly, claiming to act on behalf of Islam, killed four people who were also Jewish.

18   On 20 August 2016, in Strasbourg, a man in his sixties wearing a kippa who went out to do errands was knifed by an attacker crying 'Allahu Akbar'. Naturally, the press referred to the attacker as 'an unbalanced person'.

19   Commissioned by Luc Ferry and Xavier Darcos in 2004, the Obin Report, an X-ray of the French national education system, pointed out the difficulty of teaching the Shoah to students hyper-sensitized to the Israel-Palestine conflict. But not only the Shoah; also the architecture of cathedrals, Greek mythology, and *Madame Bovary*, seen as immoral because it is about adultery, or *Tartuffe*, because it mocks religious hypocrisy.

Chapter 10

1   Amos Oz, *How to Cure a Fanatic*, New York: Vintage, 2012, p. 68.

2   'With the creation of the state of Israel, the whole Muslim nation was lost, because Israel is a cancer that is spreading throughout the whole body of the Islamic nation, and because Jews are a virus that resembles AIDS, and that is infecting the whole world. You will discover that Jews have been the origin of all the world's civil wars. Jews are behind the suffering of nations. The day will come when everything will be taken back from the Jews, even the trees and the stones that have been their victims.' A sermon delivered on 13 May 2005 at the Great Mosque of Gaza, quoted in Küntzel, *Djihad et haine des Juifs*, p. 15.

3   Hani Ramadan, blog.tdg.ch, 23 October 2009. Tsahal is an acronym referring to the State of Israel's armed forces.

4   Robert Wistrich, *Muslim Antisemitism: A Clear and Present Danger*, New York American Jewish Committee, May 2002. Many passages in the Quran describe Jews as perfidious and malevolent beings doomed to 'debasement' in this world and a 'magisterial punishment' in the next.

The Jews have refused to accept Allah's revelation, and since the beginnings of Islam they have sought to divide and weaken it. As for the Holocaust, it is a diabolical invention, a marketing operation intended to conceal the far worse crimes committed by Zionists against Palestinians. The 11 September 2001 attacks on New York (renamed 'Jew York') were welcomed with cries of joy in many Arab countries. This anti-Semitism has, of course, been spread by Muslim immigrants in Europe and in the United States, and is found in Muslim communities in every Western country.

5   Pierre-André Taguieff, *Dictionnaire historique et critique du racisme*, Paris: PUF, 2013, pp. 525–7.
6   Edward Said, 'Diary', *London Review of Books*, 1 June 2000, pp. 42–3.
7   *El Moujahid*, 10 June 1967, quoted in Bouteldja, *Les Blancs, les Juifs et nous*. For her part, Bouteldja calls for Sartre to be shot posthumously.
8   See, for example, in the Spring 2012 issue of *Islamophobia Studies Journal*, a publication of the University of California at Berkeley, the article by Ramón Grosfoguel, 'The Multiple Faces of Islamophobia'.
9   Thomas Deltombe, *Le Monde*, 1 November 2013.
10 A talk given at the Massachusetts Institute of Technology in May 2016, sponsored by the Ecology and Justice Forum in Global Studies and Languages, on the theme: 'Is Islamophobia Accelerating Global Warming?'

Chapter 11
1   Closing speech at the meeting of the Union of Islamic Organizations of France in Lille, 7 February 2016.
2   Luc Le Vaillant, 'La femme voilee du metro', *Libération*, 2 December 2015.
3   Philippe Bernard, *Le Monde*, 29 August 2014. Quoted in Philippe d'Iribarne, 'Le déni postmoderne des cultures propres à un peuple', *Le Débat*, August 2015, p. 140.
4   In an article published on 17 August 2016, *Le Canard enchaîné* pointed out that the CCIF, an organization close to the Muslim Brotherhood that was financed, for a time, by George Soros, systematically defends imams accused

of radicalism, and that its former director, Marwan Mohammed, took advantage of his position as an editor at the Organization for Security and Co-Operation in Europe (OSCE) to do pro-Islamist lobbying, which led to his resignation. Now he swaggers alongside Salafist speakers such as Rachid Abou Houdeyfa, the imam of Brest who has said that 'those who like music will be transformed into apes and pigs', and that a woman 'who did not wear a veil had no honour and deserved to be raped'. Despite his invigorating remarks, ISIS sentenced the imam to death for apostasy because he called upon the faithful to vote and to recognize what France had given them. The wolves devour one another.

5   Hajjat and Mohammed, *Islamophobie*, pp. 33–4.
6   *Rapport sur l'intégration au Premier ministre, JeanMarc Ayrault*, December 2013, prepared by Thierry Tuot. The report proposes to abandon integration in favour of inclusion, as well as to abandon part of the French heritage and 'the most resounding, flashy, and shimmering capital letters – Rights and Duties, Citizenship! History! Achievement! French Civilization! Fatherland! Identity! France!', seen as being as ridiculous as they are anachronistic. As if Déroulède could resolve social problems! To talk about integration or assimilation is to resort to 'neo-Vichyist anathemas' (p. 13). The report is placed under the sign of a poem by Novalis celebrating 'the proud foreigner with profound eyes, a light step, and half-closed lips trembling with songs'. As beautiful as Novalis's poem might be, Thierry Tuot makes it sound like a pompous cliché straight out of advertising. Kitsch is not always where we expect to find it!
7   Isabelle Kersimon and Jean-Christophe Moreau, *Islamophobie, la contre-enquête*, Paris: Plein Jour, 2014, p. 53.
8   Ibid., p. 201.
9   *L'Express*, 4 May 2006.
10 'When I turn on the TV, I feel attacked as an anti-racist, but also as a person. I am a Muslim by culture, and recently I've said to myself every day: "What exactly is the problem? Why are we constantly put in the dock as

if we were the cause of all this country's ills?"' Rokhaya Diallo, interview with Sabrina Kassa, regards.fr, 9 May 2011. On 28 October 2010, the same Rokhaya Diallo, reacting to Bin Laden's threats demanding that France get out of Afghanistan and repeal the law banning the full-body veil, declared that 'what Bin Laden says is not false [...]. We give him reasons to threaten us.' Bin Laden had notably said that 'if France has a right to forbid free women from wearing the veil, isn't it our right to push for the departure of your invading men by cutting off their heads?'

11   Diallo, *Racisme, mode d'emploi*, pp. 51, 52.
12   CCIF, 2016 report, consultable on the association's internet site.
13   In 2015 the attacks in January correlated with an increase in anti-Muslim acts: 178 in three weeks as opposed to 133 for the whole year of 2014. But this correlation was not reproduced in the same proportions after the Bataclan attack (13 November 2015) and Nice (July 2016); only ten to fifteen more anti-Muslim acts occurred during the month, followed by another decrease afterward.
14   *Le Monde*, 3 May 2016.
15   'We are not on the brink of a civil war', wrote Jérome Fourquet in *Le Monde*, 19 July 2016. Even if 28 per cent of the French consider Islam a threat, a large majority refuses to lump all Muslims together and does not yield to violence.
16   *Libération*, 21 and 22 September 2013. Small cubes of this cheese had been marketed, in partnership with Trivial Pursuit, with the following question: 'Where did the problem of the Islamic veil appear in 1989?' The correct answer was Creil (a town about 40 miles north of Paris). Faced by the outcry, the cheese producer had to issue an apology.
17   Fourest, *Éloge du blasphème*, p. 115.
18   Isabelle Kersimon, '5 vérités concernant le collectif français contre l'islamophobie', http://islamophobie.org.
19   According to the Senegalese sociologist and diplomat Ousman Blondin-Diop, fundamentalism endangers

the Black African religious exception defined by a confluence between Arabo-Berber values and indigenous spiritual traditions based on animism, ancestor worship, shamanism, and maraboutism, as in Senegal or in Mali. Islam was able to Africanize itself by espousing pre-Islamic customs. 'Menace sur l'Islam noir', *Le Monde*, 30 May 2012.

20　Christian Fauré, 'Malaise occidental et altérité curative', *Digital Studies*, July 2011.

21　*El País*, 20 September 2006, quoted in Christopher Caldwell, *Reflections on the Revolution in Europe: Immigration, Islam, and the West*, London: Penguin, 2010, pp. 153–4.

22　Thus in 2000, the minister of the interior in the Jospin government, Jean-Pierre Chevènement, launched extensive talks that resulted in a pact signed with the representatives of French Islam. Like a good republican, Chevènement is said to have sought to include therein a clause asserting every person's 'right to change religions and convictions'. Comparing the latter to an act of apostasy, the Muslim authorities rejected the clause.

23　There are almost a million and a half Christians in Saudi Arabia, chiefly Filipino expatriates, Lebanese, Indians, and Europeans. They are forbidden to go to Medina or Mecca. No place of worship is provided for them. On 18 March 2008, *The Guardian* reported ongoing discussions about constructing a Catholic church in Riyadh. But in 2012, Sheikh Abdul Aziz ibn Abdillah, the Grand Mufti of Saudi Arabia, declared that 'all the churches in the region have to be destroyed'. The Mufti based his decision on a Hadith reporting that on his deathbed Muhammad said: 'There must not be two religions in the Arabian peninsula.'

Chapter 12

1　In *Le Monde des Livres*, 13 November 2015, Jean-Claude Milner writes, very much to the point: 'In the rejection of institutions based on ethnic or religious communities, the Caliphate [ISIS] saw an unprecedented opportunity offered to equality; it fears that Muslims might take advantage of it. Above all, it fears the spontaneous secularism of the ordinary individual: what would happen if Muslims in Europe realized that they are allowed to be indifferent in matters of religion, like everyone else?'

Chapter 13
1   Hamadi Redissi, *L'Exception islamique*, Paris: Seuil, 2004, p. 9.
2   Quoted by Antoine de Gaudemar, *Libération*, 13 February 1999.
3   John Le Carré, quoted in William J. Weatherby, *Salman Rushdie, Sentenced to Death*, New York: Carroll & Graf, 1990.
4   On the positions taken by the two sides, see the German website signandsight, 23 March 2007, 'Islam in Europe'.
5   Blog by Jean-François Bayart, 'La laïcité, nouvelle religion nationale', Mediapart, 18 August 2016.
6   *New York Times*, 25 August 2016.
7   Paul Berman, *The Flight of the Intellectuals*, New York: Melville House, 2011, p. 274. I myself engaged in a polemic with Timothy Garton Ash and Ian Buruma in 2007, on the German website Perlentaucher, directed in Berlin by Thierry Chervel.
8   On this dispute, see the excellent article by Ron Rosenbaum in *Slate*, April 2010.
9   'Les poupées Barbie de l'islam lite: exhibitionnisme et érotisme victimaires', Ouma.com, 10 February 2008.
10 The ironic expression is that of Jean Birnbaum, *Le Monde*, 2 December 2013, 'Quand la gauche antiraciste loupe la marche'.
11 Planned to appear in the original soundtrack for the film *La Marche*, starring Jamel Debbouze, alongside Disiz and Nekfeu (25 November 2013).
12 *Libération*, 9 January 2015, quoted in de Saint Victor, *Blasphème*, p. 116.
13 *Le Monde*, 8 January 2015.
14 The performance of the play *Mahomet ou le fanatisme*, staged by Hervé Loichemol in 2005 at Saint-Genis-Pouilly under police protection, was initially banned in

Geneva in 1993. At that time Hervé Loichemol accused Tariq Ramadan of having influenced this decision. The latter replied in an open letter to the *Tribune de Genève*: 'In proximity to private and sacred places, isn't it sometimes better to impose silence? It may be that the play provokes no protest or any visible mishap, but be assured that its affective consequences will be very real; it will be one more stone in the edifice of rejection and hatred in which Muslims feel they are being imprisoned.' It is more likely that in 1993 the authorities in Geneva subjected themselves to a spontaneous self-censorship.

15 According to the 'Brigade des mères' association that conducted an investigation in Sevran. France 2 (TV channel), 7 December 2016.

16 'La chasse aux barbus est ouverte à Air France', *Le Canard enchaîné*, 10 May 2016.

17 This view was severely condemned in France by Sihem Habchi, then president of Ni Putes Ni Soumises (*Le Figaro*, 5 June 2009).

18 See Meddeb, *La Maladie de l'Islam*, pp. 45 and 46.

19 On this phenomenon unique in the Near East, see Pascale Bourgaux, *Moi, Viyan, combattante contre Daech*, Paris: Fayard, 2016. When the Syrian Democratic Forces, an Arab-Kurdish alliance supported by the United States, held a press conference on 6 November 2016 to announce the beginning of the offensive to retake Raqqa, the soldier who read the communiqué was a woman who spoke with her head uncovered and with another female combatant at her side, also with her head uncovered. The symbol is enormous in that region.

20 Zineb el Rhazoui, BFM-TV Ruth Elkrief, 'Personne ne nous parle de burcalecon'.

21 On this subject, see Paul Berman, *Terror and Liberalism*, New York: W. W. Norton, 2004, Chapter 3. See also my preface to the French translation, *Les Habits neufs de la terreur*, Paris: Hachette Littérature, 2004.

22 Rodinson, *La Fascination de l'Islam*, p. 40.

Chapter 14

1   Quoted by Tidiane n'Diaye, *Le Génocide voilé*, Paris: Gallimard, 2008.

2   Pascal Blanchard, Nicolas Bancel, and Sandrine Lemaire, *La fracture coloniale: la société française au prisme de l'héritage colonial*, Paris: La Découverte, 2005.

3   Pascal Blanchard, 'Ce que la France doit aux arabes', *Le Nouvel Observateur*, 30 November 2013.

4   Sadri Khiari, *De quelle couleur sont les Blancs?*, pp. 39–45.

5   Colloquium on 'Langage et Violence' organized by the Primo Levi Association, 17 June 2011.

6   Emmanuel Brenner, ed., *Les Territoires perdus de la République*, postface by Georges Bensoussan, Paris: Mille et Une nuits, 2002, enlarged edition, Paris: Fayard, 2015.

7   French citizens resident in Algeria and Algerians who supported France during the Algerian war of independence.

Chapter 15

1   The author of this latter expression was General José Millán-Astray y Terreros. The phrase 'Death to treacherous intellectuality' was used during a lecture by the philosopher Miguel de Unamuno, rector of the University of Salamanca, in October 1936.

2   Boualem Sansal, *Gouverner au nom d'Allah*, Paris: Gallimard, 2013, p. 135.

3   Quoted in Redissi, *L'Exception islamique*, pp. 64–5. The medical metaphor is used by Abdelwahab Meddeb in his fine book *La Maladie de l'Islam*, where he attributes the explosion of fundamentalism to unrestricted access to the letter of the Quran, which used to be protected by strict interpretative conditions, but is now manipulated by semi-educated individuals eager to take revenge.

4   Quoted in Birnbaum, *Un silence religieux*, pp. 56, 57.

5   'The portmanteau word behind this slogan, which is on target, is supposed to be "radicality", an atemporal phenomenon that has allegedly remained unchanged

from the anarchists of the nineteenth century down
to Direct Action, passing by way of the Italian Red
Brigades, the Baader-Meinhof gang in Germany, and
ISIS today. It is said to be merely a nihilist itch, peculiar
to adolescence, to destroy society, now garishly daubed
with Islamist green after having been communist red
and fascist brown at an earlier time.' Gilles Kepel, *La
Fracture*, Paris: Gallimard, 2016, p. 139.

6   Sansal, *Gouverner au nom d'Allah*, p. 130.
7   Mathieu Guidère says that in this they are being faithful
     to the Prophet's thought, which 'evolves, over time, from
     a position of moral and spiritual preaching in Mecca
     toward a position of political and religious direction of
     the Muslim community in Medina'. 'Petite histoire du
     djihadisme', *Le Débat*, Gallimard, May–August 2015,
     p. 38.
8   Quoted by Caldwell, *Reflections on the Revolution in
     Europe*, p. 242.
9   Ibid., p. 244.
10   Cf. Hamadi Redissi, a professor of law at the University
     of Tunis, *Le pacte de Nadjd, ou Comment islam sectaire
     est devenu l'islam*, Paris: Seuil, 2007. The Nadjd Pact
     was the alliance signed in 1774 between the House of
     Saud and Mohammed ibn Abd al-Wahhab, a doctrinaire,
     stringent Bedouin inspired by the Kharijites, a fanatical
     sect during the first years of the Hegira. Wahhabism
     won out in 1932 when the sovereigns reunified Saudi
     Arabia and adopted this version of Islam as their official
     doctrine. See also Henry Laurens, quoted in Küntzel,
     Djihad et haine des Juifs, p. 8.
11   *Activités royales*, 'Discours de SM le roi à l'occasion du
     63ᵉ anniversaire de la révolution du roi et du peuple',
     maroc.ma, 20 August 2016. The kingdom of Morocco
     is separate from the Maghreb in so far as the king,
     anointed with a prophetic heritage, directs a veritable
     'bureaucracy of belief' (Mohamed Tozy) and presides
     over the Higher Council of the Ulama, which has a
     monopoly on the production of religious meaning.
     Moroccan Islam follows the Maliki school, and has
     experienced a major development of Sufi brotherhoods.

12   Cf. for example Ghaleb Bencheikh, 'La passivité des musulmans devant le sauvagerie est inquiétante', *Le Monde*, 3 August 2016. Bencheikh, a French citizen of Algerian origin, is a learned student of Islam and a physicist.

13   Aboubaker Djaber Eldjazaïri was a preacher in Medina, born in 1921. His book was published in French by the Maison d'Ennour in 1997.

Chapter 16

1   Friedrich Nietzsche, *Human, All Too Human*, trans. A. Harvey, Part II, 'The Wanderer and his Shadow', #344.

2   'Les deux blasphemes', *Libération*, 6 March 2006.

3   In 2014, the Indonesians also elected a Chinese Protestant, Basuki Tjahaja Purnama, as mayor of Jakarta, a twofold transgression that enraged the extremists. In late 2016, he was put on trial for blasphemy. Tolerance has its limits.

4   In a rather worrisome report commissioned by the Institut Montaigne at the IFOP and published in September 2016 under the direction of Hakim El Karoui, two realities emerge regarding Islam in France: a silent majority practises its religion without major conflicts with French society, while a minority of 30 per cent, mainly young people, is attracted by fundamentalism to express its revolt against France and adopts an attitude favouring secession. For the latter, there is said to be a 'divine urgency' to impose in the public sphere halal food, the veil, and the segregation of women. One figure is astonishing: 88 per cent of the people surveyed would agree to shake a woman's hand. After a century and a half of feminism, such a response might make us wonder...

5   Quoted in Küntzel, *Djihad et haine des Juifs*, p. 124. Hassan al-Banna, *Five Tracts of Hassan AlBanna*, trans. Charles Wendell. Berkeley: University of California Press, 1978, p. 7.

6   Jean-Pierre Machelon, 'Combats d'hier, laïcité d'aujourd'hui', *Le Débat*, May–August 2015, pp. 87, 88.

7   On this subject, see Mathieu Bock-Cote's very good analysis in *Le Multiculturalisme comme religion politique*, Paris: Cerf Éditions, 2016, pp. 214, 215.

Chapter 17

1   Lévi-Strauss, *The View from Afar*, p. 24.
2   *Le Figaro*, 11 February 2015.
3   On this theme, see Pierre Manent, *Situation de la France* (Paris: Desclée et Brouwer, 2015), where the author, in a very British-American spirit, argues with conviction for allowing Muslims to enjoy their mores: namely by accepting all their demands regarding the relation between men and women, alimentary prohibitions (notably banning pork from cafeterias), wearing the veil, segregation in swimming pools, on beaches, and in hospitals: 'The relations between the sexes are a subject of such complexity and delicacy that it would probably be unreasonable to condemn a civilization on this question.' We should accept Sharia as the juridical basis of French Islam. In a final concession to the secular spirit, the author does ask that polygamy and the full-body veil be banned. But why refuse believers these two privileges when everything else has been surrendered to them?
4   Farhad Kohsrokhavar, 'Le Djihad et l'exception francaise', *New York Times*, 19 July 2016.
5   Farhad Kohsrokhavar, 'Ce fondamentalisme laïque qui fragilise la France', *Le Monde*, 9 September 2016.
6   Guy Sorman, *Le Point*, 29 September 2016.
7   Montesquieu, *De l'esprit des lois*, XII, 4, quoted in de Saint Victor, *Blasphème*, p. 48.
8   Benedict XVI, homily, Christmas 2011.
9   According to a World Bank report published in October 2016 and based on leaked ISIS internal data concerning almost 4,000 persons, the majority of ISIS's officials are far from being uneducated. They do not come from the problem neighbourhoods but from the universities. Poverty is not a factor in radicalization. Twenty-five per cent of these officials had gone to a university, 43.3 per cent had completed a secondary education.

An interesting detail: the proportion of candidates for suicide missions increases with education. According to the Unité de coordination de la lutte antiterroriste (UCLAT) in France, 67 per cent of the young candidates for jihad came from the middle classes, and 17 per cent from higher socio-professional categories (2016 statistics). Here we are far from the sociologizing litany about the wretched of the Earth!

Chapter 18

1   Erdoğan spent four months in prison for uttering these words.

2   Quoted in Alexandre Devecchio, *Les Nouveaux Enfants du siècle*, Paris: Cerf Éditions, 2016, p. 13. Régis Debray made this statement after the attacks on *Charlie Hebdo* and the Hyper Cacher supermarket.

3   René Guénon, *La Crise du monde moderne*, Paris: Gallimard, 1946, pp. 90, 91.

4   'Muslims make mistakes, Christians go astray, Jews are puzzled, and Zoroastrians lose their way. The inhabitants of the Earth are of two sorts: those with brains, but no religion, and those with religion, but no brains [...] All religions are equally mistaken' (Abu Al-Ma'arri, *Luzumiyat*). Al-Ma'arri has been translated into French by Adonis and Vincent-Mansour Monteil. His works are forbidden in some Arab countries and celebrated in others, including Tunisia.

5   Saul Bellow, 'My Paris', *New York Times*, 13 March 1983.

6   Along the same lines, Jean-Pierre Chevènement, the former minister of education who was asked to set up a foundation for Islam in France, told *Le Parisien* in mid-August 2016: 'The advice I give Muslims in this difficult period is to be discreet.' He added that this suggestion held for all denominations.

Chapter 19

1   Mehmed Çelebi was the Ottoman Empire's first ambassador to King Louis XV of France, in 1721. His diary served as the inspiration for Montesquieu's *Les Lettres*

persanes and was also the origin of a mutual infatuation between the two countries.

2   Al-Afghani was an Iranian intellectual who inspired *Al-Nahda*, the Awakening, a renaissance movement in the Arab world in the late nineteenth century.

3   Cited in Rodinson, *La Fascination de l'Islam*, p. 101.

4   Edmund Husserl, *La Crise de l'humanité européenne et la philosophie*, trans. Paul Ricoeur, Paris: Aubier, 1977, p. 49.

5   In September 2016 an anti-Wahhabi meeting was held in Chechnya under the aegis of the tyrant Kadyrov. It brought together a large number of religious dignitaries, including Sheikh Ahmed el-Tayeb, the imam of Al-Azhar University in Cairo, a Sunni Muslim authority, which constitutes an encouraging sign. The scholars, partisans of a 'quietist' Islam, did not mention Salafism in their definition of Sunnism, thereby infuriating Riyadh.